# TRANSFORMATIONAL LEADERSHIP

## A STUDY OF GENDER DIFFERENCE BETWEEN PRIVATE AND PUBLIC SECTOR ORGANISATIONS

# DR. MANPREET KAUR BHATIA

Copyright © Dr. Manpreet Kaur Bhatia
All Rights Reserved.

# Contents

# PREFACE

Transformational leadership is a leadership style where one or more persons engage more persons engage with another in such a way that leaders and subordinates raise one another to higher levels of motivation and morality. Transformational leaders enhances the personal and group improvement, share inspiring organizational visions, objective, motivation, morale for important goals. According to Bass (1999), transformational leaders attempt and succeed in raising colleagues, subordinates, followers, clients or constituencies to a greater level of awareness about issues of consequence.

These leaders are having a strong vision supported by a will to act. There are many examples from business, politics or other fields, who have been doing very well in terms of bringing revolutionary change among the members. Further, there are few women leaders as well. However, one can easily find the difference in proportion of male vis-a-vis female leaders in many categories. However, now the women are making their mark in terms of transformational leadership. Be it Kiran Majumdar Shaw, Arundati Bhattacharya or Chanda Kochar, women are setting the standards of excellence in the areas, which were once considered for men. This study aims at developing insight on employee retention is relevant in present business context. This study is divided into five chapters:

**The Chapter 1** consists of Introduction of the topic, rationale of the objectives, Transformational Leadership, Gender differences in leadership style and social relevance of the study.

**The Chapter 2** consists of Review of Literature in lieu of the factors of Transformational Leadership.

**The Chapter 3** deals with Research methodology consists of research design, data collection instrument, tools to measure questionnaire, statistical analysis tools etc.

**The Chapter 4** consists of data analysis & interpretations and deals with different aspects of research essential for the study. The study is descriptive research in order to examine the difference between male and female leaders in terms of transformational leadership style and also the perception of subordinates towards transformational style of their leaders. It deals with the objectives and hypotheses of the study. The sample is based on the primary sources. Through SPSS Package (20.0 version) T-Test was used for the analysis, interpretation of data and results.

**The Chapter 5** presents the discussions, conclusion on the factors based hypotheses testing results. It also explains the the suggestions reached by the researcher on the basis of results of study and also scope for the further study.

**Bibliography** discusses all the authors and their works which are duly acknowledged. The references used to complete this study were compiled under the bibliography in alphabetic order. Kindly see the bibliography for the references.

*Author.......,*

# Acknowledgements

In presenting this thesis, I would like to acknowledge the assistance of several persons for their inspiration, support and help received from different sources, is a matter of heart warming remembrance. First and foremost, all praise is due to God for bestowing me with health, knowledge and patience to complete this work.

I take this opportunity to express my deep sense of gratitude and sincere thanks to my Research Guide Dr. Jitendra Sharma [Associate Professor, Acropolis Faculty of Management & Research, Affiliated to Devi Ahilya Vishwavidyalaya, Indore] and the Co-Guide Dr. Jyoti Sharma [Reader, Institute of Management Studies, Devi Ahilya Vishwavidyalaya, Indore] for their valuable guidance and support. I find no words to express my deep sense of gratitude to our respected guides for their excellent supervision, constant encouragement and constructive criticism right from the choice of the research problem, till the submission of the thesis.

I am grateful to Dr. Babita Agarwal and Dr. Manpreet Kaur Rajpalfor their belief and faith upon me, moreover continue inspiration and moral support which enabled me to make continuity in research work.

From the bottom of my heart, I am grateful to my respected parents for providing moral support, encouragement providing me all necessary facilities for the successful completion of this endeavour and inspiration every time; my brother Ishmeet Singh Bhatia and relatives for always supporting me. I want to thank all my school and college friends and all my well-wishers, who have helped me for this study directly or indirectly.

## ACKNOWLEDGEMENTS

I consider it is my privilege to place on record the help, support and encouragement received from respondents who took their initiative in filling the questionnaire in spite of their busy schedule. I am thankful for their valuable inputs in the form of suggestions and recommendations in my research, without their participation, it would have been impossible to complete this task.

I owe my loving thanks to my dear and near ones they have lost a lot due to my research. Without their encouragement and understanding it would have been impossible for them to finish this work. Above all I thank again the Almighty and my loving Father and My Mother who has been the sole source of spirit and strength to me, in my entire endeavour in this venture.

*"Dr. Manpreet"*

# I

# INTRODUCTION

## 1.1 CONCEPT OF LEADER

Leaders are not born leaders are made if any person has will power, he can become an effective leader good leader develop never-ending process of education self-study, experience and training. Good leaders are working and studying continuously to improve their leadership skill.

The world "leaders" appeared in the English Language year 1300 (Oxford English Dictionary, 1933) Leadership is an influences process in which leaders influences other to carry out their objective and they guide, organisation in the way that make it more effectively.

A leader is one who charts a purpose, inspires trusts and confidence, goes all the way for the team and shows the way. A enlists the team for missions, backs them for mission, backs them and takes pride in their performance, achievement and growth. Position is a manager supervisor and leads in the organisation they give leader to certain task and objective. Only power does not make you leader it simply make a boss, they give order for their subordinates leadership makes a follower want to achieve their goal.

When person has deciding respect a person as a leader that person does not think about your attributes, that person observes what you're doing in the position of leadership and what is your working style after that person decide are you honourable are not and trusted leader or a self services person when leader is self-service leader so he is not effective because they are subordinates not fellow them only they fellow their order. India is a land of many Great Leaders who ruled and developed the country effectively, they also protected our country. In India leaders play a very important role to develop the country, many leaders made history and did very important historical changes in country. Leader like Mahatma Gandhi, Indira Gandhi, Jawahar Lal Nehru, Lal Bahadur Shastri played very important role to changing the perspective of other countries towards India.

Leaders are said to be different from ordinary managers. They focus up on to the articulation of mission, direction setting, vision, and strategic thinking. Managers concentrate on the administrative functions of achieving the goals, administering policies and procedures, and monitoring and controlling (Krantz, 1990, p.188). Leading is the most important function of management after planning and organizing. Through guiding and motivating Managers have to lead their subordinates. To perform essential tasks leading involves motivating, directing and influencing and motivating employees. **Abraham Lincoln**, **Dr. Ambedkar** etc are world known political leaders while J. R. D. Tata and S. L. Kirloskar are known leaders in the business world. Most of them are used in the present century to replace the word "leader" the meaning of which is basically regarded a "person who guides".

*Leadership is the influencing method of leaders and followers to achieve organizational aims through changes. Dhirubhai Ambani (28 December 1932 - 6 July 2002) Dhirubhai Ambani is the most famous business leader of India. We called him Business Magnate. First Dhirubhai started import export business and then Reliance Industries and after years of hard work his dream to make the world's largest oil refinery of the world was completed in 1999 Jamnagar, Gujarat. Ghanshyam Das Birla (April 10, 1894 - June 11, 1983) G.D Birla is the founder of the Aditya Birla group; we called him A shrewd Businessman because he left his family business and started cotton dealership. His business was success than he started many industries like paper mill , sugar factory, than car factory etc. and started a commercial bank now mill, known as United Commercial Bank which is still working by the name of UCO Bank. Now Aditya Birla group operates in more than 33 countries and employs over 133,000 with an annual turnover of more than USD 35 billion. Ardeshir Godrej (1868 - 1936). He knew as Lock master of India. He is the founder of the Godrej group of companies. One day in the morning he was reading news paper and read a news burglary in Bombay is increased and locks aren't proving useful as they should be. After that He saw business opportunity and started to research about making locks and the locks of their company famous in the world, now the Godrej group also famous for real estate, appliances, security, FMCG products etc.*

**Table 1.1:** Top ten Business Leader in India

| S. No. | Name of Person | Duration | Known name | Industries |
|---|---|---|---|---|
| 1. | Dhirubhai Ambani | 1932 – 2002 | Business Magnate | Reliance Industries |
| 2. | Ghanshyam Das Birla | 1894 – 1983 | Shrewd Businessman | Aditya Birla group |
| 3. | Ardeshir Godrej | 1868 – 1936 | Lock-master of India | Godrej group |
| 4. | Govindram Seksaria | 1888 – 1946 | Cotton King of the World | Cotton King |
| 5. | Bhai Mohan Singh | 1917 – 2006 | Pioneer of the Indian Pharmacy Industry | Ranbaxy |
| 6. | Jamsetji Tata | 1839 –1904 | Father of Indian Industry | Tata group of companies |
| 7. | Jehangir Ratanji Dadabhoy Tata | 1904 –1993 | Father of the Indian Aviation Industry | Tata Steel |
| 8. | Kailash Chandra Mahindra | 1894 – 1963 | Sophisticated and Meticulous | Mahindra and Mahindra |
| 9. | Verghese Kurien | November 26, 1921 | The man behind the White Revolution of India | Amul |
| 10. | Walchand Hirachand Doshi | 1882 –1953 | Dare Dreamer | Hindustan Shipyard Limited |

*[Source: Times of India, 2013]*

## 1.2 LEADERSHIP

"Leadership is a word on everyone's lips. The young attack it and the old grow wistful for it. Parents have lost it and police seek it. Experts claim it and artists spurn it, while scholars want it. Philosophers reconcile it (as authority) with liberty and theologians demonstrate the compatibility with conscience. If bureaucrats pretend they have it, politicians wish they did. Everybody agrees that there is less of it than there used to ". (Bermis and Nanus, 1985)

Every organisation needs strong and able leaders for its success. Leadership is an important aspects and essential ingredient of management. Leadership is an abstract quality in a human being to induce others (his followers) to do whatever they are directed to do with zeal and confidence. It is a ability or quality or ability of an individual to persuade others to seek defined objectives enthusiastically. Do you know that what makes an organisation effective? Some management analysts believe that the basic difference between a successful and an unsuccessful organization is its leadership. In most cases, the failures are caused by poor leadership. Therefore, an organization's leaders are major determinants of its success or failure (Katzm Kahn, 1978). In other words we can say, "The successful organization is one respect the former are characterizing by dynamic and effective leadership" (Hersey & Blanchard, 1977).

Peter Northouse (2001) defines leadership as a process whereby one individual influences a group of individuals to achieve a common goal.

Organisation would be merely a confusion of people and machine without leader. "Leadership is the lifting of man's visions to higher sights; the raising of man's performing to a higher standard, the building of man's personality beyond its normal limitations." (Peter – Drucker 1970). The leader is a dynamic force of the organisation that designs, execute, coordinates and control all the function of organisation, i. e., planning, executing, organising, directing and controlling. Leadership inspires; creates confidence; help the team mates to give their best for achieving the objectives. Koontz and O'Donell 1955, have touched the very essence of leadership in saying that, "Subordinates want to be led and led effectively. They will work just hard enough to get by if there is little or no leadership; with effective leadership, they will work with zeal and confidence towards the peak of their capabilities."

So any organisation or business organisation need a leader, so the organisation may get the maximum out of the efforts of the subordinates who may be willing to contributes towards the organisation goal. In a business organisation, managers at all types, by whatever name called, are leaders because they all have subordinates whose efforts are canalised in a definite direction. As leaders, they have to show the way to the subordinates towards the attainment of organisations goal and to lead the groups towards them. In reality, organisation compete by means of their leaders that by their products. A leader gives a company the life which creates the products and innovations that it sells.

### 1.2.1 MEANING OF LEADERSHIP

The word "leader" appeared in the English language at about the year 1300 (Oxford English Dictionary, 1933) and the "Leadership" at about 1800 A.D. (Stogdill, 1974). So the leadership has mainly three meaning –

First, it is an attributes of a particular position. Second, it is trait of personality or characteristics of a particular person. Too thirdly, leadership is a kind of behaviour, it is the way or style of influence others. In simple words, leadership is a process of directing others towards the accomplished of goal. It is the ability to influence the behaviour of others to accomplish particular goals. Leadership is an essential ingredient for successful organisations. Leadership is an important abstract quality of leader that set apart a successful organisation from an unsuccessful one. Without leadership an organisation is nothing more than a mass of men, machine, and materials.

Leadership is not merely the personal quality or characteristics acquired by a person but it is much more than that, his relationship with his followers and others.

### 1.2.2 DEFINITIONS OF LEADERSHIP:

The following are the views of different authors on leadership:

1. Ivancevicti, Szilagyi and Wallace (1993), define "the relationship between two or more people in which one attempts to influence the other toward the accomplishment of some goal or goals."
2. According to Keith Davis (1967:96), "Leadership is the ability to persuade others to seek defined objectives enthusiastically. It is the human factor which binds a group tighter and motivates it towards goals."
3. A Great Management Guru, Peter F.Drucker (1970) defines, "Leadership is the lifting of man's visions to higher sights, the raising of a man's performance to a higher standard, the building of a man's personality beyond its normal limitations."
4. (Bennis, 1959) says; the presence of a particular influence relationship between two or more persons.
5. According Hollander and Jullian 1969; directing and coordinating the work of group members.
6. Fiedler 1967 defines in interpersonal relationship in which others comply because they want to, not because they have to.
7. Merton 1969 says, transforming followers, creating visions of the goals that may be attained, and articulating for the followers the way to attain these goals.

8. Bass (1990)adds that leadership is not only viewed as a process, but also as a role that people play to maintain their relationships. In other words, when leadership is viewed as a process.

9. Burns (1978)states "Leadership continues to be the most observed and least understood phenomena on earth ".

Thus, leadership is the process and the art influencing the behaviour, attitudes and activeness of people to the work willingly and enthusiastically towards the accomplishment of group goals. Leadership exits in every organisation whether formal or informal. It may be anywhere and in every situation: where someone tries to influence the behaviour of others, there is leadership.

Transformational leadership is a type one who inspires organisation success by profoundly affecting followers beliefs in what an organisation should be as well as their values, such as justice and integrity. Transformational leaders are generally passionate, active and enthusiastic. Not only are these leaders concerned and involved in the process; they are also focused on helping every member of the group succeed as well. In its ideal form, it creates valuable and positive change in the followers with the end goal of developing followers into leaders.

**Definitions of Transformational Leadership**

1. Transformational leaders are considered to be enthusiastic and optimistic when speaking about the future, which arouses and heightens their followers' motivation (Dubinsky, Yammarino, & Jolson, 1995).

2. Transformational leadership has become one of the most widely-studied leadership styles due to its emphasis on changing workplace norms and motivating

employees to perform beyond their own expectations (Yukl, 1989).

3. Transformation leadership highlighted satisfying followers inferior stage needs established on a price benefit exchange procedure which happened among followers and leaders (Ogbonna & Harris, 2000; Xenikou & Simosi, 2006).

4. Transformational leaders encourage the team to do better, make them more efficient so that they can achieve more and go of the organization to the followers (Jassawalla & Sashittal, 2002; Prather & Turrell,(2002).

Transformational leadership enhances the motivation, morale and performance of followers through a variety of mechanisms. These include connecting the follower's sense of identity and self to the mission and the collective identity of the organization; being a role model for followers that inspires them; challenging followers to take greater ownership for their work, and understanding the strengths and weaknesses of followers, so the leader can align followers with tasks that optimize their performance. It is related to the impact that the leader has on followers. Transformational leaders earn trust, respect and high regard from their followers.

### 1.2.3. A HISTORICAL PERSPECTIVE ON LEADERSHIP

Leadership is complex and multidimensional. What makes a leader effective is a question which cannot be answered easily. Many researchers, particularly by behavioural scientists, were carried out to find out the answer to this question. For these various theories have been developed to analyze and explain "what makes an effective leader." There are four approaches to studying leadership. The trait approach emphasizes the personal qualities of leader. The style approach or leader behaviour approach is concerned with identifying the kind of leader behaviour that enhances the effectiveness of subordinates. The contingency approach concerns the impact of situational factors upon leaders and followers. Finally, there is the new leadership approach which emphasizes the leadership vision and charisma. Each of these is described in more detail below.

### 1.2.4. FUNCTIONS OF LEADERSHIP

Leadership is a dynamic and constructive force in any organisation. It plays a crucial role in the success and survival of an organisation. It is the crucial factors that help individuals to identify their goals. Functions of leadership are as follows:-

### FIGURE 1.1: FUNCTIONS OF LEADERSHIP

*[Source: Book, Management Principal and Practices, Parag Diwan]*

- **Guide and inspires or motivates**: - An effective leader guides and inspires or motivates his group members to work willingly for achieving the goals. He makes every effort to direct and channelize all energies of his followers to the goal oriented behaviour. He creates enthusiasm for higher performance among his followers.
- **Determination of goal**: - A Leader plays a crucial role in laying down goal and policies of his group or the institution. He acts as a guide in setting organisational goal and polices.
- **Boosts morale**: - Morale refers to the attitude of employees towards organisation and management and will to offer voluntary cooperation to the organisation. Morale is an internal feeling of a person. A good leader can arouse will to cooperate among the employees.
- **Creates Confidence and enthusiasm**: - A good leader creates confidence among his group members. He/she does so by providing psychological support and infuses the spirit of enthusiasm among them.
- **Develops team spirit**: - A good leader constantly tries to develop team sprit among his group members/followers. He/she inculcates a sense of community of interest. He/she provides a satisfying work climate by harmonising individual and group goals. Thus, a leader reconciles goals and creates team spirit.
- **Create vision and initiative:** - It has been rightly said, where there is no vision, people perish. Leaders give

vision to their followers which, in turn, create initiative and enthusiasm among them. The followers use this vision and initiative to take up challenging tasks.

- **Transform potential into reality**: - Effective leader can transform potential or dream into reality. Leaders can identify, develop, channelize and enrich the potentials existing in an organisation and its people.
- **Representation**: - A leader represents his group members. He/she is the connecting link between his group members and the top management. He/she carries the views and problems of his group members to the concerned authorities and tries to convince them.
- **Development and use of human recourses**: - An effective leader can develop and utilise human resource in a most effective way. A leader can influence the activities and behaviour of his follower of his followers to contributes their best.
- **Facilitates change**: - Leaders can induce change. They are the instrumental in conceiving and managing change. They introduce change by convincing their followers about the positive effects of the change.

- **Ensures survival and success of the enterprise**: - No doubt that leadership plays a vital role in the survival and success of an enterprise. The quality of leadership goes a long way in the success and survival of an enterprise. Without effective leadership, many well established enterprise.
- **Resolves Conflicts**: - Leaders play crucial role in resolving the conflicts arising in the group. He/she does it by harmonising the diverse intense interests of group members and the organisation.

## 1.3 LEADERSHIP THEORY

Various theories have been developed to analyze and explain 'what makes an effective leader.' The important approaches to leadership are as under-

- Trait Theory
- Situational/Contingency Theory
- Power and Influence Theory
- Behaviour Theory

## FIGURE 1.2: APPROACHES TO LEADERSHIP THEORY

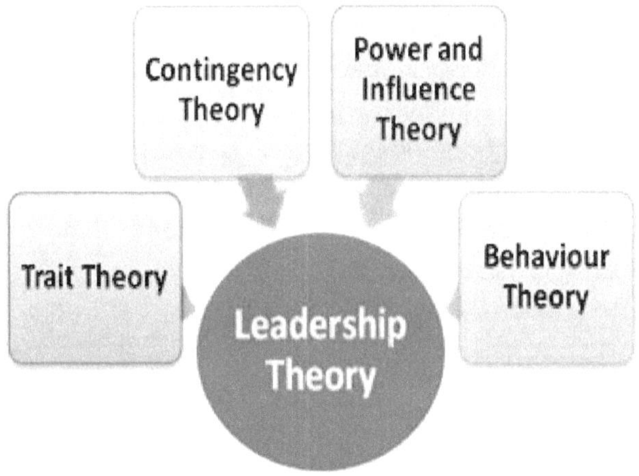


*[Source: Book, Management Principal and Practices, Parag Diwan]*

- **The Trait Theory**

The trait theory of leadership is a classical theory focuses upon leadership personal qualities. This approach is based on the assumption that leaders could be identified by specific traits or characteristics. The aim of the trait approach then was to identify the personal attributes of leaders which differentiated them from non-leaders. In other words researchers asked themselves what kind of personal qualities make some leaders. There are three broad types of trait which have been addressed by the literature. First are physical elements such as height, weight, appearance and age. Second are ability characteristics such as intelligence, scholarship and knowledge, knowing how to get things done, and fluency of speech. Third, other personality features such as self-confidence, inter-personal sensitivity and emotional control.

Hundreds of trait studies were carried out during the 1930s and 1940s but according to Stogdill (1974) the massive research effort failed to find any traits that would guarantee leadership success.

The reason behind Failure of the trait approach following:

i.   First providing only a list of traits and skills found to be productive, did not help in understanding leadership.
ii.  Secondly, trait approach failed to tell what these leaders actually do in performing their day to day leadership tasks.
iii. Thirdly, measurement used by researchers in this approach did not include psychological scaling (Smith and Peterson, 1990).

This theory include following approaches-

- The great man theory
- The personality theories

- **The Great Man Theory :-**

Thomas has said ": The theory of the world is but the biography of great man." There have been great man leaders in business world- Rockefeller, Carnegie, Ford etc. The great-man view emphasizes 'who' the person is and what makes the person great. Researcher's tried to find out the specific traits that characterized "the great person." This approach implies that we can learn how to become effective leaders by studying great people and emulating their characteristics. This approach lost its value with the rise of behavioural sciences. These made it clear that people are not born with traits, other than inherited physical features.

- **The Personality Theories**-

The great man theory (that leaders were born not made) finally gave way to this more realistic trait approach. Many studies in the past several decades have been conducted to isolate personality traits common to many leaders. This approach is based on the premise that there are certain personality traits that are not completely in born, but can also be acquired through learning and experience. These traits are supposed to differentiate leader and non leader. It emphasizes what a person is in terms of personality traits. Research is still continuing for that set of universal leadership traits that will assure success.

- **Situational Approach on Theory**

The trait approach in effect explained certain desirable characteristics or traits which an effective leader must possess, but the theory fails to suggest that one who possesses the particular mix of traits shall or shall not be leader. On the other hand, the behavioural approach attempted to explain various practices or style available to a leader to discharge his leadership functions, but this again failed to indicate which style available to a leader to discharge functions, but this again failed to indicate which style is the best which leader should follow to be an effective leader in all circumstances. Both these theories ignored one important variable, i.e. situation which greatly influences the trait or behaviour. Various researches made doing 1970s established that it was not the trait or behaviour of a leader that matter but it was a particular situation in which a particular trait or behaviour is effective or ineffective. A Leader may prove effective in one situation change. One glaring example is that of Winston's Churchill who was a very successful Prime Minister during the World War II. However, he proved quite ineffective afterwards when the situation change. The theory, thus, advocates that it is a particular situation that helps develop leadership and from which leaders emerge. Trait or behaviour may be supportive elements.

Ohio State University research has given four situational variables that affect behaviour:

- The Cultural environment
- Difference betweeen individuals
- Difference between jobs
- Difference between Organisations

Thus, situational theory of leadership stresses how leadership differs with situational variables or why person in a particular situation is successful unsuccessful.

### · Power and Influence Theory

This approach is based on social psychology. This theory connotes that leadership is an interpersonal influence. It is a positive exchange between the leader and follower in order to achieve group objectives. It is a two way influence relationship. It indicates that subordinates affect leaders and their behaviour as much as leaders and their behaviour affect subordinates.

Thus, according to this view, leadership is an exchange process between the leaders and followers. The leader provides more benefit than costs for followers. This creates his influence. Hollander and Julian state, "The very sustenance depends upon yielding to influence on both sides."

### · The Behavioural Theory

When it became clear that the trait theory was unable to explain what caused effective leadership, the researchers, in the late 1940s, began to study the behaviour of leaders.

The trait theory seeks to explain leadership on the basis of what leader are and not what leaders do but the behaviour theory focuses on the style or the behaviour of the leader. It concentrates on what leaders actually do on the job.

Ohio State University concluded that major dimensions of leaders' behaviour involved two factors - consideration and initiation.

Consideration basically refers to the consideration to followers. This means the group leader understand to the group members, shows concern for their welfare, is friendly and approachable, expresses appreciation for good work, treats subordinates as equals, increases subordinates' work and maintains their self esteem, reduces inter-personal conflict and put subordinates' suggestions into operation. Initiation define the task related behaviour, as initiating activity in the group, organizing it, coordinating tasks, defining the problem for the group and the way the work is to be done. The initiation of structure includes such leadership behaviour as planning activities, facilitating goal achievements, providing feedback for the group, maintaining standards and meeting deadlines, deciding in detail what should be done, and how establishing clear channels of communication, organizing work tightly, structuring the work context, provide a clear-cut definition of role responsibility. A number of problems have been identified in the behavioural approach. Firstly, inconsistent finding, that is, the magnitude and direction of correlation between consideration and initiating styles and various outcome measures were highly variable. Also, some correlations failed to reach statistical significance (Korman, 1966).

Secondly, Absence of situational analysis behavioural approach studies failed to include in their research situational variables, that is, including variables which moderate the relationship between leader behaviour and various outcomes (Korman, 1966). Thirdly, Measurement problem, for example, consideration measure seems to be affected by influence affect. Rating of leaders found to be contaminated by subordinates implicit theory (Bryman, 1992). Finally, the problem of causality, that is, does the style of leader influence various outcomes or does the leader adjust his/her style in response to group performance.

## 1.4 Transformational Leadership

"Recognizes and exploits an existing need or demand of a potential follower... (And) looks for potential motives in followers, seeks to satisfy higher needs, and engages the full person of the follower" ... Burns (1978).

Transformational leadership is a leadership style where one or more persons engage more persons engage with another in such a way that leaders and subordinates raise one another to higher levels of motivation and morality. Transformational leaders enhances the personal and group improvement, share inspiring organizational visions, objective, motivation, morale for important goals (e.g. Bass, 1985;Kouzes and Posner, 1987). According to Bernard Bass, "Transformational leaders attempt and succeed in raising colleagues, subordinates, followers, clients or constituencies to a greater level of awareness about issues of consequence" (*Leadership and Performance Beyond Expectations*, 1985). It provides ideas as to what a leader should be in transforming environment Vision statements create discussion. It can be used in recruitment, selection and promotion, and training and development programs. Transformational leadership, behaving in ways that bring out the best in individuals and organizations, may be a more androgynous style, calling for the best in both masculine and feminine sex-typed behaviour (Hackman 1992). The best example of transformational leadership are- Mahatma Gandhi, Mother Teresa, Martin Luther King, Nelson Mandela they are demonstrated a form of transformational leadership that was based on values, motivation, morality etc. According to Bass's Theory of Transformational Leadership define transformational leadership is-

- ○ Raising followers' level of consciousness about the importance and value of their objectives.
- ○ Getting followers to transcend their own interest for the good of the organization and their team.
- ○ Moving followers to address higher level needs for organization.

Transformational leadership can inspire positive changes in those who follow it; Transformational leaders are generally energetic, enthusiastic, and passionate. Not only are these leaders concerned and involved in the process they are also focused on helping every member of the group success.

**According to Bass (1985)**Transformational leadership can be defined based on the impact that it has on followers. Transformational leaders, Bass suggested, garner trust, respect, and admiration from their followers.

**Exactly said by Bass (1985)** – "the transactional leaders work within the organisational culture as it exists; the transformational leader changes the organisational culture".

### 1.4.1 HISTORY OF TRANSFORMATIONAL LEADERSHIP

**James Burns** introduced the concept of transforming and transactional leadership (1978)

• A process in which leaders and followers help each other advance to a higher level of motivation and morale

• Differentiated between management and leadership claiming the differences are in characteristics and behaviours, and established two concepts: - transforming leadership - transactional leadership

· Transformational leadership creates significant change in the lives of people and organizations.

· It redesigns perceptions and values, and changes expectations and aspirations of followers

· Dependent on the leader's personality, traits and ability to change through example, articulation of an energizing vision and challenging goals.

· Provides a moral example of working towards the benefit of the individual, team and organization.

· Transforming and transactional leadership are mutually exclusive styles.

## 1.4.2 THE COMPONENTS OF TRANSFORMATIONAL LEADERSHIP

Bass also suggested that there were four different components of transformational leadership.

### FIGURE 1.3: TRANSFORMATIONAL LEADERSHIP MODEL

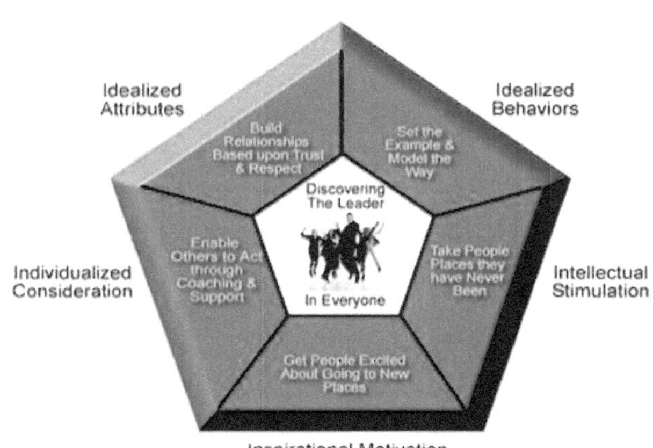


*Source: - Compiled by author according to Bass M. (1988)*

- **Individual consideration:-**

It is the most outstanding component of transformational leadership is the leader's individualized consideration. According to Bass and his colleagues (Yammarino, Spangler & Bass, 1993), all leaders' use of individual consideration is a crucial element in followers' achievement of their full potential via a close consideration of their developmental needs. Individual consideration reduced to the ability of person to person analysis of followers its main aiming to study their wishes, needs, values and abilities in the right way. It involve team orientation, teaching, responsibilities, appreciations of others, creativity, responsibility etc.

- **Idealized influence (Attributed and Behavioural):-**

The transformational characteristic of idealized influence is based on earlier conceptualization of charisma (e.g. House, 1977). Idealized influences express the ability of making and develop the confidence in the leader and appreciating the leaders by his followers, which forms the basic development change in any organization. The leader is able to communicate a sense of power and confidence in higher values and beliefs.

- **Inspirational motivation:-**

The transformational leadership inspires people toward the different latest ideas or objectives through inspirational motivation. The leaders provide ability of transformational leadership which qualifies leader as a figure which inspires and motivates the followers to appropriate behaviour. It involves-

- Motivating term
- Highlighting motivational term
- Motivational conversation
- Highlighting positive outcomes
- Developing the shared vision
- Motivate people to become a part of organization culture etc.

- **Intellectual stimulation**

It is one type of ability of transformational leaders. It plays important role in the transformational process of organization. The leaders provide intellectual stimulation to followers. They simulate the efforts their followers as creativity and new inventions, in providing intellectual stimulation, the leader is said to orient followers to "and awareness of problems, to their own thoughts and imagination, and to the recognition of their beliefs and values" (Yammarino & Bass, 1990). Intellectual stimulation plays important role in process of organization. They give creative solution of any problems.

## 1.5 TRANSACTIONAL LEADERSHIP

"Approaches followers with an eye to exchanging one thing for another" ... Burns (1978)

"Pursues a cost benefit, economic exchange to met subordinates current material and psychic needs in return for "contracted" services rendered by the subordinate "…. Bass (1985)

The transactional style of leadership was first described by Max Weber in 1947 and then by Bernard Bass in 1981. It is also called managerial leadership, its aim to focus on the role of organisation supervision, and group performance. It was first described in by sociologist Max Weber, and further explored by Bernard M. Bass in the early 1980s.

Transactional leadership is one who guide and motivates his follows in the direction of established goals by clarifying role and task requirements. Transactional leadership involves exchange relationship between the leader and the followers. Traditional theory of leadership, Ohio State studies, Fiedler's model and Path Goal theory are all transactional in nature. On the basis of his research finding, Bass concluded that in many instances, transactional leadership is a prescription for mediocrity and that transformational leadership leads to superior performance in organisation facing demands for renewal and change. He suggested that fostering transformational leadership through policies of recruitment, selection, promotion, training and development will pay off in the health, well – being and effective performance of today's organisations.

Robbins defined the transactional leadership as "Leaders who lead primarily by using social exchanges for transactions" (Robbins, 2007).

Managers will continue to face the challenge of changing their organisation primarily because of the accelerating trend to position organisations to be more competitive in the global business environment. Therefore, transformational leadership will probably get increasing attention in the leadership research by the behavioural scientists.

The leader values the relationship between managers and subordinates as an exchange, in return to you give something for him or her. If subordinates perform well, they receive reward. When they don't perform well, a punishment may apply (Hartof & Koopman, 1997).

Transactional leadership is basically based on the fact that punishment or rewards is totally based on the person's performance. Even though researchers have criticized the limitations and functions of it, it is still used by many employers. More companies seem to be adopting transactional leadership to increase the performance and productivity of its employees (Avolio & Bass, 1999).

- **Contingent reward**

Contingent reward is one type of process in which we follow exchange process between leaders and followers in which efforts by followers is exchanged for specified rewards. In the contingent rewarding behaviour, leaders give the particular specific assignments what needs to be done in exchange for getting the rewards. An example would be the relationship between a parent and child negotiating how much TV the child can watch after doing his/her homework assignment. If the child studies well for the day, then he/she will get the chance of watching TV as the exchanged reward of his effort (Hartof & Koopman, 1997).

Contingent reward behaviour makes a strong relationship with leader effectiveness. The present studies examined the impact of contingent rewards on perceived autonomy, which was measured in terms of reports (Avolio & Bass, 1999).

Transactional leaders link the goal to rewards, clarify expectations, provide necessary resources, set mutually agreed upon goals, and provide various kinds of rewards for successful performance. They set SMART (specific, measurable, attainable, realistic, and timely) goals for their subordinates.

- **Active management-by-exception**

After the goals are set Active management by exception occurs and they are not being met so that corrective action may be required. It also consists of some items that encourage the leader focusing on monitoring task execution for any mistakes before any problems arise. For example: Mistakes of products cost time in terms of revisions and customer complaints. Managers should correct those mistakes before their consequences occur. This would save some time whereas it should increase the productivity in the organization (Avolio & Bass, 1999). Transactional leaders monitoring actively work of their subordinate and taking corrective actions on their subordinates on deviations from standards.

- **Passive management-by-exception**

Passive management-by-exception types of rewards are totally connected to the performance of the employee. If employee give their proper efforts towards the organisation so it recognized by the rewards.

Passive management-by-exception type of leaders intervenes only when employee is not given standards of the work or organisation not satisfy their work so organisation can even use punishment as a response to unacceptable performance. For example: If a soccer player does not perform well continuously, the team manager can start him as a substitute in the next games. This would impact player's budget as most soccer players are getting incentives such as bonuses for each game he plays. This is a certain punishment for the player (Rowold, 2006).

· **Laissez-faire Leadership**

Laissez-faire leadership defines a type of behaviour in which leaders display a passive indifference towards their followers (Moss & Ritossa, 2007). Laissez-faire leaders incline to move out from the leadership role and offer little direction or support to followers (Kirkbride, 2006), Laissez-fair leadership give the least possible guidance to their subordinates, and try to control through less obvious means. They believe that people excel when they are left alone to respond to their responsibility. The present study examined the relationship of gender to self reported and observes the rated transformational leadership. Three hypotheses were derived, based on previously cited research:

1. There will be no difference between men and women head of the any Institution in transformational leadership behaviours.

2. What is the effect of transformational leadership and laissez-faire leadership style are predictors of leader style.

Robbins (2007) explained the laissez-fair style as "Abdicates responsibilities avoid making decisions". Similar Luthans (2005), defined laissez- fair style as "Abdicates responsibilities avoid making decisions".

The concept of laissez was also given by Osborn as "Abdicates responsibilities and avoiding decisions" (Osborn, 2008).

Bass (1981) noted that the laissez-faire leader:

...................does nothing unless asked by colleagues and even then may procrastinate or fail to response, 'he laissez-faire leader will be non active or reactive. ... The laissez-faire leader may work alongside

Subordinates or withdraw into paper work. Decision will be avoided rather than shared.

## FIGURE 1.4: MODELS ON TRANSFORMATIONAL STYLE OF LEADERSHIP

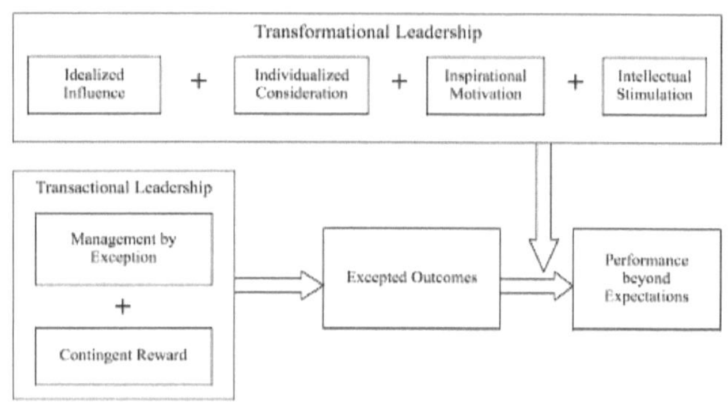


**Source :** Bass & Avolio (1990, p.231)

## 1.6 TRANSACTIONAL OR TRANSFORMATIONAL LEADERSHIP

The greatest think of all is that leading and managing, punishing for great change and yet keeping the organisation ticking (kakabadse and kakabadse, 1998). Context is the intervening variable between the two form of leadership – transformational and transactional. The power of context is substantial, for context helps individuals form their attitudes and perspectives regarding life, work, people and the organisation. Singh and Bhandarkar (1990)intensively studied five Indian transformational leaders who had affected substantial changes in the culture and performance of their organisations. The changes seemed to have resulted from the introduction of more open communication, participative targets-setting, teamwork, empowerment, result-orientation and risk taking, as well as concern both for tasks and the people.

One of the factors influencing the effectiveness of leadership is the leader's perception of unexplored positive opportunities in the large environment.

Followers are more likely to accept a person's leadership if they consider his leadership behaviour to be culturally appropriate and in agreement with their own culture values. kanungo and conger (1993). Thus in a traditional organisation which prescribes conservative mode of behaviour for its members.

(kakabadse and kakabadse, 1998) hold that there should be a balance between transformational and transactional elements of leadership. Transformational leadership is more attractive than the day to day grind of routine, maintenance – type activities offered by transactional leadership.

## 1.7 PUBLIC SECTOR IN INDIA

Initially Public sector is a part of individual state, which deals with the production, delivery as well as allocation of different goods or services by its citizen or government. These sectors consist of administration of urban planning, organisation of national defence and delivery of social security.

In India the corporation or company which is owned by government is undertaken in Public Sector Company. If a Union government or any territorial government owns a share of 51% or more is mostly regarded as a company of public sector.

In today's era the public sector in these country includes sectors like oil and petroleum industries, steel industries, coal industry, banking industry, jute industry, food industry, thermal power industry, insurance industry, telecommunication industry, service industry, agriculture industry, aviation industry, manufacturing industry, mining industry, electricity industry, engineering industry (Light and medium) etc. To name a few of the famous public sector companies in India are.

- Air India Limited (A. I. L.)
- Airports Authority of India (A. A. I.) Limited
- Akaltara Power Limited
- Andaman and Nicobar Islands Forest and Plantation Development Corporation
- Balmer Lawrie and Company Limited
- Bank of India (B. O. I)
- Bengal Chemicals and Pharmaceuticals Limited (B. C. P. L.)
- Bharat Coking Coal Limited (B. C. C. L.)
- Bharat Dynamics Limited (B. D. L.)
- Bharat Electronics Limited (B. E. L.)
- Bharat Heavy Electricals Limited (B. H. E. L)
- Bharat Petroleum Corporation Limited (B. P. C. L.)
- Bharat Sanchar Nigam Limited (B. S. N. L.)
- Coal India Limited (C. I. L.)
- Electronics Corporation of Tamil Nadu Limited (E. L. C. O. T.)
- Hindustan Aeronautics Limited (H. A. L.)
- Indian Institutes of Technology (I. I. T.)
- Indian Oil Corporation Limited
- Life Insurance Corporation of India (L. I. C.)
- Mahanagar Telephone Nigam Limited (M. T. N. L.)
- Mazagon Dock Limited (M. D. L.)
- Modern Food Industries (India) Limited (M. F. I. L.)

- National Institutes of Technology (N. I. T.)
- N. T. P. C. Limited (Earlier National Thermal Power Corporation)
- Nuclear Power Corporation of India Limited (N. P. C. I. L.)
- Oil and Natural Gas Corporation (O. N. G. C.)
- Power Grid Corporation of India Limited
- State Bank of India (S. B. I.)
- Steel Authority of India Limited (S. A. I. L.)
- Tamil Nadu Electricity Board (T. N. E. B.)
- Tamil Nadu State Transport Corporation (T. N. S. T. C.)
- The Jute Corporation of India Limited

There was no public sector was introduce in India in late 1947. Only some state manage undertake government salt factories etc. And only in some areas like telegraph, Railways posts, the port trusts, the ordinance and aircraft factories government were worked. In 1996-97 236 central public sectors undertaken without considering banks and these increased investment in central public sector from 1951 the no of industrial and commercial has increased from 5 units in 1950-51 to 236 units in 1996 to 1997 and the capital investment has increased by 29 cores to 2020.2 billion in 1996 – 1997. To know the role of public sector we must have an idea about its size in the context of the Indian economics.

Organisationally there are four types of public sector enterprises:-

1. Managed by independent boards

2. Departmentally Managed

3. Organised as Companies. The company form of organisation is the most common.

4. Run as public corporations

Public sector also play vital role in contribution to national income. The public sector doubled its share in national income in period of 1960-1999 in real terms.

| Plan | Percentage |
|---|---|
| II Plan | 54.6 |
| III Plan | 63.7 |
| IV Plan | 60.3 |
| V Plan | 57.6 |
| VI Plan | 52.9 |
| VII Plan | 47.8 |
| VIII Plan | 36.5 |
| IX Plan | 33.4 |

## TABLE 1.2: SHARE OF PUBLIC SECTOR IN TOTAL INVESTMENT

The above table shows the investment in this sector is that after having reached the peak during the third plan, the share of public sector, in total investment in each of the plans has however, been on the decline.

### 1.8 PRIVATE SECTOR IN INDIA

The component of the economy that is not state forced, and is run by persons and companies for profit. All the private sector organisations encompass for-profit in businesses that are not owned or operated by the government. Public sector Companies and corporations are run by government, while charities and other non profit organizations are part of the unpaid sector. In the private sector most jobs are held. All the **companies, corporations or businesses and** organisation which owned by group and private citizensinstead of the state or government that is**Private sector organizations.**The private sector is prepared up of every commercial business that is not owned or operated in any form by the government. Private sector is the largest employer of society with the huge popular of employees working for privately owned companies.

"Under private enterprises, the capital is owned principally by individuals or non-governmental organisations and its major decisions, especially on investment, the scale of production and prices are chosen by the firm itself, with government providing a framework for the activity of the enterprise rather than participating in the firm's decision-making". (Rutherford, 1992) Individual persons are only responsible to form the private organisations. The one and only aim behind the formation of this organisation is to be paid its share out of the market in a perfect and imperfect competition. These type of organisations working under a government prescribed rule of business but free from government regulations, procedures and interference.

## 1.9 GENDER DIFFERENCE FOR TRANSFORMATIONAL LEADERSHIP

Gender is derived from Latin word, genus it means kind or soft. Gender difference in leadership style has been of great interest in research. In the planning and managing activities, personal responsibility female score higher point in compare to men but males are strong in commercial focus, strategic vision, and personal impact. The word gender is used to describe the quality, roles and responsibilities of women and men, girls and boys, which are socially constructed. Gender is related to how we are perceived and expected to think and act as women and men because of the way society is organized, not because of our organic differences. (World Health Organisation, 2009). In this study we also examine the difference between men and women leaders with respect to their transformational leadership style. Women adapt to leadership that is more democratic and less of autocratic styles than men are (Eagely, Johannesen-Schmidt, & Engen, 2003). Several studies say that male are task oriented and women are people oriented. Several studies in the research shown that compare to male female tend to be more transformational. Subordinates of the head of the organisation rated the dimensions use of transformational leadership behaviour from five different categories. Some data indicate that women leaders employ different style then men. (See Grant, 1988; Kabacoff, 2001; Karau & Eagly, 1999; Kim & Shim, 2003; Rosener, 1990). Women tend to be somewhat more transformational than male. One might propose anti-feminine bias and disadvantage as a plausible explanation for finding that women are somewhat more transformational and therefore more likely to make effective leaders (Bass, Avolio, & Atwater, 1996). Compare to male, female have to be better leader in the same position of level of success and responsibility as male. In other hand, in the Industries, government sector and military also promoting large number of females into the leadership position. In the first level and middle management also have opened the door for female Gottlied also completed the study on nursing administrator in veteran's hospitals and emerge with challenging contrary findings. The perception of effective leadership in influenced by variables such as race, culture, gender (Lober, 1994) In Eagly and Johannesen-Schmidt analysis and women and men's leadership style they found women rated slightly higher on three of the transformational leadership scales. Men were found to be higher in transactional leadership scales. As women show more supportive behavior as compared to men (Gregory, 1990; Eagly & Karau, 1991) women have less informal contact that male so women are do their work very effectively that men. 201 Norwegian companies found in the research that the leadership styles differed amongst the sexes for specific tasks and situations.

They state that women and men do not differ in their ability to perform operational tasks, but rather bring a different perspective to strategic decision-making through their increased sensitivity to others (Nielsen & Huse, 2010). A research amongst 7280 leaders conducted by Zenger Folkman shows that women excel at most leadership competencies. Respondents were requested to rate men and women based on criteria of 16 competencies, where the largest gaps in favour of women were found in taking initiative, practicing self-development, integrity and honesty and driving for results (Zenger Folkman, 2012). Another research finds that there is no gender difference in effectiveness of board members but there are gender differences in certain behaviours (Yukl, 2002).

# II

# LITERATURE REVIEW

There has been some commendable research work done in the subject matter. Some of the major areas of research covered are as follows:

**A study by Gibson et al (1995)**[1] provided concern about potential gender differences across countries. At least among this sample of leaders, country of origin does not appear to influence the divergence in male and female emphasis on at least two dimensions of leadership: goal setting and interaction facilitation. Australians indicated less emphasis on interaction facilitation and more emphasis on a directive style than did managers from the other countries in this sample. This may be due to Australia's geographic isolation.

**Deanne N. Den Hartog, Jaap J.** Van **Muijen** and **Paul L (1995)**[2], evaluated to test the factor structure of the MLQ as developed by Bass & Avolio. The MLQ-8Y was analysed using data collected in Dutch organizations. Seven hundred employees from eight organizations rated their leader's behaviour with the MLQ. First, an indication of the internal consistency of the scales developed by Bass is reported. The results of subsequent factor analyses show that the three types of leadership can be

organizations. Seven hundred employees from eight organizations rated their leader's behaviour with the MLQ. First, an indication of the internal consistency of the scales developed by Bass is reported. The results of subsequent factor analyses show that the three types of leadership can be found in the data; however, the scales found here are slightly different from Bass' scales. Especially, the transactional and laissez-faire scales have been altered on theoretical and empirical grounds. The adapted version of the MLQ covers the domain with fewer items.

**Ivana Simić (1998)**[1]studied Transformational leadership represents the essential quality for successful management of transformational organizational changes. It is about the quality that, in fact, so-called transactional management has missed to bring to an end of the transformational cycles with efficiency. In that sense, the success in realizing transformational organizational changes means that the key people in an organization (managers) develop sets of appropriate skills and attributes that are characteristic to so-called transformational leaders.

**Bernard M. Bass (1999)**[2]explained about the interests of the members of any type of organisation and organization in the work in organisation. In these contrast they explained about transformational leadership and transactional leader, transactional leader who practises contingent reinforcement of followers, the transformational leader inspires, intellectually stimulates, and is individually considerate of them. Transformational leadership may be directive or participative. Requiring higher moral development, transformational leadership is recognized universally as a concept. Furthermore, they explained women leader more transformational than male. Although a six-factor model of transformational/transactional leadership best fits a diversity of samples according to confirmatory factor analyses, whether fewer factors are necessary remains an open question.

**Gretchen Spreitzer and Kimberly Hopkins Perttula (2001)**[1] This research examines how the effectiveness of transformational leadership may vary depending on the cultural values of an individual. They developed the logic for why the individual value of traditionality (emphasizing respect for hierarchy in relationships) moderates the relationship between six dimensions of transformational leadership and leadership effectiveness. The hypotheses are examined on leaders from Asia and North America. Final result indicate support for the moderating effect of traditional values on the relationship between four dimensions of transformational leadership (appropriate role model, intellectual stimulation, high performance expectations, and articulating a vision) on leadership effectiveness.

**Tracey T. Manning (2002)**[2] explores about the gender and organisational level of interact; they explores that how gender and organisational level interact to influence rating of leadership. They also define about work satisfaction and argue that transformational leadership permit women to simultaneously carry out leadership and gender roles. in this study they explain similarities in male and female managers and transformational leadership and work satisfaction male and female top managers saw them self as more transformational leaders while their rated less transformational than average for the sample. Lower managerial level want to upgrade them self as a leader but their ratters perceived them as higher than average in transformational leadership. At last the result were discussed in term of how organisational status, feedback process, potential obstacles to women's accurate assessment of their leadership abilities and experience.

**Alice H. Eagly and Mary C. Johannesen, Marloes L. van Engen (2003)**[3] studied about the transformational, transactional, and laissez-faire leadership styles. They found female leaders were more transformational than male leaders. They also studied that engaged in more of the contingent reward behaviours that are a component of transactional leadership. Male leaders were generally more likely to manifest the other aspects of transactional leadership (active and passive management by exception) and laissez-faire leadership. Although In these contest it were as very small differences between male and female leaders, the implications of these findings are encouraging for female leadership.

**Boatwright et al (2003)**[4] investigated the influence of psychological variables upon female college students' aspirations for leadership positions in their future careers. Data were gathered from 213 undergraduate women. Results demonstrated that connectedness needs, gender role, self-esteem, and fears of negative evaluation accounted for a significant amount of the variance in predicting college women's leadership aspirations. Implications of findings for improving leadership development initiatives are discussed.

**Ken W. Parry and Sarah B. Proctor-Thomson (2003)**[5]have attempted to test hypothesised relationships between manifestations of leadership, culture type and effectiveness in the public sector. They were Using comparative structural equation modelling, Two consecutive national leadership surveys were conducted to investigate organisational factors that are relevant to the pressing management issues present in the uncertain and turbulent environment of today's public sector. Measured constructs include Transformational / transactional organisational culture, climate for innovation, individual transformational leadership, team transformational leadership, and team and organisational outcomes. Support was found for the indirect and direct effects of transformational leadership on outcomes through its influence on transformational/transactional culture and climate for innovation. Implications for leader development and for the development of productive cultures are considered.

**Neubert and Palmer (2004)**[6] evaluated the strengths and weaknesses of more women moving into positions of influence as much as it is to encourage organizations to consider this trend as an opportunity for transforming leadership roles. Eagly (2005) studied relational view of leaders' authenticity by arguing that much more is required of leaders than transparently conveying and acting on their values. Achieving relational authenticity requires that followers accord leaders the legitimacy to promote a set of values on behalf of a community. Only under such conditions can leaders elicit the personal and social identification of followers that can enhance the success of a group, organization, or society.

**Hakan Erkutlu (2006)**[7] focused on the leadership behaviour on organisational and leadership effectiveness. These study explained the aspect of leadership in the neglected hospitality, This study provide the connectivity to understand the nature of the leadership behaviours and effectiveness. In this study he was talking about leadership effectiveness of boutique hotels. In this study they were taking 722 subjects total 60 managers and 662 non managerial employees from different hotels, they were used MLQ for designing the data and explained that there are significant leadership behavious and both organisational and leadership effectiveness .

**Alexi Matveev and Elean Lvina** (2007)[8] focused on relationship between Transformational leadership and the cross cultural communication competence. They wanted to explain about how national culture orientation and cross culture communication affect the leadership and transformational leadership framework and dimensions. In this research they said that charismatic or value based leadership dimension the most effective perceived to the leadership style. They said that to understand better effective transformational leadership new theoretical framework are needed. At the last they conclude that the along cultures view effective leaders as charismatic, team oriented, participative and humane. They believed that scholars and practitioners will benefit from further investigations of transformational leadership using the cross culture communication competence frame.

**Hassan (2008)**[9] tried to fill the gap that existed in the literature on gender and leadership behaviors in community development because women contribution is getting bigger but too often they are not documented. Analysis of data showed that leadership understanding and style employed by women leaders is participatory or collaborative in nature and this is in line with some of the finding from other studies in women led organization in other countries.

**Jacqueline Whittred (2008)**[10]investigated qualitative exploration into the transformational leadership styles of senior police women ways of work in which women are doing leadership. They also investigate that ways in which police culture presents barriers to the career development of women. This research analyse that male have some conflict to accepting women in police roles and has caused women to doubt their skill and their right to growth during the policing ranks. They explored the ways in which the encouraging women involved in this study are breaking down barriers through transformational leadership. There was a clear identification that the progression of more women and minority groups within the police organisation would be likely to improve the quality of service to diverse communities due to the diversity perceptions influencing policy and strategy.

**Roger J. Givens (2008)**[11] focused on Transformational leader's behaviour to inspire followers to accomplish more by concentrating on the follower's values and helping the follower align these values with the values of the organization. These study focused to investigate the impact of the transformational leadership style on organizational outcomes and the personal outcomes of the follower. They examined organizational citizenship behavior/ performance, organizational culture, and organizational vision organizational outcomes and personal outcomes empowerment, job satisfaction, commitment, trust, self-efficacy beliefs, and motivation of the follower. By understanding the impact of transformational leadership on these outcomes, transformational leaders can influence employee behaviour so that the behaviour has a positive impact on the organization. In this study they investigate that organization select assist by those people who has leadership qualities which one helpful in growth and develop the organisation as well growth and development of follower of the organisation.

**Mahmood Ahmad Bodla and Muhammad Musarrat Nawaz (2010)**[12] investigated leadership styles among teaching faculty members of higher education institutes and universities in different cultures, occupations, organizational settings. In this study seeks to determine the leadership style of regular faculty members employed by public as well as private sector higher education institutes and universities. The results revealed that the faculty members in both public and private sectors were practicing transformational and passive/avoidant leadership styles to the same extent. On the other hand transactional leadership style was being experienced significantly with higher degree by the faculty members in private sector than those in public sector. This study define that transactional leadership is more motivational in public sector organisations. This research analysis that In transformational leadership public and private sector teachers are not statistically different. Conclusion that the employees in both sectors have same degree of transformational leadership. Since there exists significant difference in the degree of transactional leadership, hence it can be concluded that public sector teaching faculty has higher level of transactional leadership than those in private sector. The analysis of the responses also discloses that teaching faculty in public and private higher education institutions have same level of passive/avoidant leadership.

**Hassan, Rasool A. Fuwad, Bashir A. Rauf, Azam I.(2010)**[13] evaluated the effectiveness of transformational leadership in training and discussed the role of training motivation in explaining the training effectiveness .They were using a true experimental design. The studied reveal a significant and positive effect of transformational leadership training on employees' satisfaction with the trained supervisors. Furthermore, trainees' (supervisors) motivation towards a Transformational leadership training program significantly and positively affects the attitudinal outcomes. This study focus the understanding the role of training program in motivational way in transformational leadership. They also explain the impacts of role of training motivation in transformational leadership.

**Thomas W. Kent, Carrie A. Blair, Howard F. Rudd and Ulrich Schuele (2010)**[14]examined the transformational leadership behaviors to differences between men and women leaders. Subordinates of the leaders rated the frequency of use of transformational leadership behaviours from five different categories. The five behavior categories and the instrument used (The Leader Behavior Inventory or LBI). Generally, it was found men and women do not differ in their general perceptions of others as leaders. it was also found that men and women leaders behave as leaders in the same way.

**Judeh (2010)**[15] studied transformational leadership by the study of gender differences in private universities. He examined the gender differences in transformational leaders' behaviors from the standpoint of both self and subordinates` ratings. Some researchers studied the transitional–transformational leadership styles in Jordan.

**Phondej et al (2010)**[16] sought to contribute to the academic literature of female leadership development. The conceptual model provides clarity for design of future empirical studies focused on the conditions and factors associated with successful female leadership in Thailand.

**Alpha and Vincent (2011)**[17] focused on the differences between female and male managers related to strategy execution and organizational performance. In a study by Munley (2011) the impact culture has on leadership was determined. It gives a comprehensive review of cultural differences in leadership and emphasizes the importance of understanding cultural differences between countries by examining the work of Hofstede and the GLOBE (Global Leadership Organizational Behavioral Effectiveness).

**Muhammad Jamshed Khan and Naeem Aslam and Muhammad Naveed Riaz (2012)**[18] examined the role of transformational, transactional, and laissez-faire leadership styles in predicting innovative work behavior among bank managers of Rawalpindi and Islamabad. Multifactor Leadership Questionnaire (MLQ; Bass & Avolio, (1990) and Innovative Work Behavior Scale (Butt, 2006) were used for data collection. Study showed that transformational and transactional leadership style positively predicted innovative work behavior whereas laissez-faire leadership style negatively predicted it and transformational and laissez-faire leadership style but inconsistent for transactional leadership style.

**Mahfuz Judeh (2012)**[19]investigated the Transformational leadership behaviours. This research indicated male and female transformational leadership behaviour, they show there was a significant difference between female and male leader's behaviours, in these male leaders scored higher on intellectual stimulation and second part of the research shown No significant differences between male and female transformational leaders regarding idealized influence, inspirational motivation, or individual consideration. At last they indicated that there was significant difference between female and male transformational leaders on intellectual simulation, the results did not support gender differences in the overall transformational leader's behaviours.

**H. S Sandhu and Kanwaldeep Kaur (2010)**[20] examined the relationship between transformational leadership behaviour of Indian bank managers and organizational commitment of their subordinates. It articulates the role of socio-cultural and organisational context within the dynamics between transformational leadership and organisational commitment. A sample of 660 bank employees working in public and private sector banks located in northern India participated in the study.

**Boris Groysberg (2013)**[21] explores about gender differences in leadership and business on the basis of decision science principles. This research informed ministers at the Tenth Women's Affairs Ministerial Meeting (10WAMM), on how to generate enabling surroundings as policy makers, to know the requisite traits and strategies that have successfully nonstop women in leadership positions and in the boardrooms. This research firstly explained about business background female leaders and after that they explained about the decision science theories thorough impression of gender differences in the individual and professional area, they gave main focus towards women in organisations.

**Joris van der Voet (2013)**[22] studied that the specific context of public organizations may have consequences for the management organizational change. This study examined to what extent different change approaches and transformational leadership of direct supervisors contribute to the effective implementation of organizational change in public organizations, and to what extent the bureaucratic structure of public organizations makes the implementation of organizational change. The implementation of an organizational change in a Dutch public organization is studied using quantitative methods and techniques. The results indicate that bureaucratic organizations may effectively implement organizational change with both planned and emergent change approaches. The contribution of transformational leadership depends on the type of change approach and organizational structure. Transformational leadership behavior of direct supervisors contributes little to planned processes of change, but is crucial in emergent processes of change in a non-bureaucratic context. Although the literature on change management mostly emphasizes the leadership of senior managers, the leadership role of direct supervisors should not be overlooked during organizational change in public organizations.

**Nasiha Begum, Farzand Ali Ja And Saif-Ud-Din Khan (2013)[23]** examined transformational leadership, gender role orientation and leadership effectiveness of male and female leaders within the context of education and health departments in Pakistan and Turkey. This research is based on gender – male and female and three leadership styles that was Transformational, Transactional and Laissez Faire, region (Pakistan and Turkey) and department, (Education and Health). They were taking four hundred male and female leaders in education and health departments In this 184 questionnaire were returned from Pakistan and 120 sample respondents contributed from Turkey. Among 12 factors (Multifactor Leadership Questionnaire 5x short Form), nine factors were employed to evaluate components of leadership style, while the remaining three factors were labelled as an outcome measures. There found to be but small differences in the leadership styles (transformational, transactional & laissez faire) of males and females. In comparison to transformational and transactional leadership styles, males and females both scored higher on transformational leadership style as compared to transactional leadership style. The score of laissez faire leadership style remained below of both the transformational and transactional leadership styles.

**Rupinder Kaur (2014)**[24]determined the perception of employees towards transformational and transactional leadership behaviour across private and public sector banks. It also aimed to determine whether such perceptions vary depending on the socio-demographic variables. Data was collected from 535 employees working in private and government sector banks in Chandigarh region. Study indicated that perception of employees towards transformational leadership behaviour does not differ but this is not the case in transactional leadership behaviour, where employees of public sector banks have more positive perception towards transactional leadership than employees of private sector banks. Perception of employees towards leadership behaviour varied according to marital status and work experience but did not vary according to gender, age, qualification and level of management. A positive perception of employees towards leadership behaviour (transformational and transactional) invests more effort in their tasks when they get motivated and inspired to excel their performance.

**Aarti Deveshwar and Indu Aneja (2014)**[25]the study explored the attention on the most popular leadership style used currently. This study focuses on the existing literature on transformational and transactional leadership style and they also examine the cross – cultural dimensional model given by Greet Hofstede. In this study they focus on two type of objective- Comparative study of Transactional and Transformational Leadership Style, Determine the cultural factors affect the leadership style. In this study they focus on different type of study which done on cross culture and they support that Transformational Leadership style is much better than transactional leadership style. we can also say that Transformational Leadership style is an extensive style and new style of the Transactional Leadership style.

**Naga Sai Sindhura Lakshmi Chaluvadi (2015)[26]** studied about values and attitude of women being a leader. In this research they tried to explained about what's causing hindrance to women expansion focusing first and foremost, if there exists any differences in the leadership styles employed by male and female leaders. They explorer about, "Do women really make better androgynous leaders?" based on several Inferences. This research focused on the morals and attitudes of women as a leadership positions. They also discussed about effect of external variables such as the corporation structure, work force and necessity of improvement on the gender in the leadership role And They compared men and women as leaders, in the context of groups, organizations and nations. They proved on the basis of large evidences women possess more transformational and transactional and participative leadership styles that their male counterparts.

# III
# RESEARCH METHODOLOGY

After the collection of research data, an analysis and interpretation of result is necessary. The purpose of analysis is to build up a sort of empirical model where the relationship involved is carefully brought out so that some meaningful inferences can be drawn. Analysis of data is to be made with reference to the purpose and objective of the study and its possible bearing on the facts that are to be revealed.

### 3.1 SIGNIFICANCE OF STUDY

Research is a plan to fulfil the objectives and test the hypothesis or assumptions. Every research consists of some concrete objectives along with hypothesis and the modus operandi of the action plan. With data collection, the plan gets the firsthand information, which gets supplemented with secondary data and results are drawn. Research in management lays the foundation for decision-making in various functional areas. The common steps of research are- defining the problem, designing the research, collection of data, analysis of data, its interpretation and implications of the findings. In this chapter the researcher has explained the research process which has been carried out to concrete facts about to examine the differences on various parameters on the transformational style of leadership between men and women.

The sampling units, method of sampling and a specific population should be defined clearly. A universe or population is the sum total of all elements having some common features like age, gender, income, marital status, designation, experience in the present profession, qualification, industry sector etc. An element is a part of the unit on which information has to be collected and it offers the standard for analysis. In this research study, the researcher has studied the impact of gender differences with respect to private and public sectors.

Gender is related to how we are perceived and expected to think and act as women and men because of the way society is organized, not because of our organic differences. Women tend to be somewhat more transformational than male. One might propose anti-feminine bias and disadvantage as a plausible explanation for finding that women are somewhat more transformational and therefore more likely to make effective leaders.

## 3.2 RESEARCH GAP AND RATIONALE OF STUDY

The existing research mentioned in previous chapter has highlighted many types of leadership. The following research gaps could be identified after review of the research work:

1. The literature reveals that many of the good research studies have been conducted on the various types of

leadership transactional, transformational and laiseez faire but a very few studies were conducted on the specific factors of transformational leadership style. This study was carried on to discuss the factors of transformational style and also to examine the gender differences in private and public sectors.

2. Men were found to be higher in transactional leadership scales. As women show more supportive behaviour as compared to men. Hence, it is imperative to study the attributes of transformational leadership style.

3. It is stated that women and men do not differ in their ability to perform operational tasks, but rather bring a different perspective to strategic decision-making through their increased sensitivity to others.

4. It is proposed that anti-feminine bias and disadvantage as a plausible explanation for finding that women are somewhat more transformational and therefore more likely to make effective leaders.

5. Transformational leaders are the extraordinary leaders who engage with followers, focus on higher the order intrinsic needs and raise consciousness about the significance of specific outcomes and new ways in which those outcomes might be achieved. The followers have blind faith on their leader if they perceive that the leader has a vision and a determination.

6. The working environment differs in private and public sectors. So this study is undertaken to examine the differences in various attributes such as; open communication, delegation, nurturing, autonomy, teamwork, conviction in self, decision making skills, conflict management, attitude to risk taking, commitment, performance oriented etc.

This study is an attempt to bridge the gap in context with the above issues. It has been undertaken from the viewpoint of males and females in all the aspects of demographic characteristics. A representative sample of respondents those who were leaders and subordinates were considered in this study. Further, the study has attempted to know the transformational style of leaders and subordinates perception towards the style of their leaders.

### 3.3 STATEMENT OF PROBLEM

"TRANSFORMATIONAL LEADERSHIP AND GENDER DIFFERENCE IN PRIVATE AND PUBLIC SECTOR ORGANISATIONS."

### 3.4 OBJECTIVES OF STUDY

The purpose of the research was to study the transformational leadership in the wake of gender difference in private and public sector organisations. Other objectives were as follows:

i. To determine the style of transformational leadership between male and female leaders on the basis of parameters.
ii. To explore the transformational leadership style of female leaders.
iii. To explore the assertiveness style of female leaders.
iv. To distinguish the leadership style of female leaders with male leaders.
v. To explore the subordinates' opinion about female and male transformational leadership styles.

### 3.5 HYPOTHESES OF THE STUDY

To maintain constancy hypotheses are translated from objectives of study. It is the statement which is meant for the purpose of testing the logical and empirical outcomes of the research. When tested through statistical tools, it can either be proven right or wrong (i.e. accepted or rejected). Hypothesis testing paves the way for the results and conclusions. To fulfil the objectives, null hypotheses were framed which were tested using statistical tools.

These null hypotheses were as follows:

**$H_{01}$:** There is no significant difference in transformational leadership approach between male and female leaders as perceived by them.

There is no significant difference in transformational leadership approach between male and female leaders as perceived by their subordinates.

$H_{03.1}$: There is no significant difference in Open communication approach between male and female leaders as perceived by leaders.

$H_{03.2}$: There is no significant difference in Open communication approach between male and female leaders as perceived by subordinates.

$H_{04.1}$: There is no significant difference in Delegation style between male and female leaders as perceived by leaders.

$H_{04.2}$: There is no significant difference in Delegation style between male and female leaders as perceived by subordinates.

$H_{05.1}$: There is no significant difference in Conviction between male and female leaders as perceived by leaders.

$H_{05.2}$: There is no significant difference in Conviction between male and female leaders as perceived by subordinates.

$H_{06.1}$: There is no significant difference in Team working spirit between male and female leaders as perceived by leaders.

$H_{06.2}$: There is no significant difference in Team working spirit between male and female leaders as perceived by subordinates.

$H_{07.1}$: There is no significant difference in Decision making skills between male and female leaders as perceived by leaders.

$H_{07.2}$: There is no significant difference in Decision making skills between male and female leaders as perceived by subordinates.

$H_{08.1}$: There is no significant difference in Attitude towards risk taking between male and female leaders as perceived by leaders.

$H_{08.2}$: There is no significant difference in Attitude towards risk taking between male and female leaders as perceived by subordinates.

$H_{09.1}$: There is no significant difference in Conflict management approach between male and female leaders as perceived by leaders.

$H_{09.2}$ There is no significant difference in Conflict management approach between male and female leaders as perceived by subordinates.

$H_{010.1}$ There is no significant difference in People development style between male and female leaders as perceived by leaders.

$H_{010.2}$ There is no significant difference in People development style between male and female leaders as perceived by subordinates.

$H_{011.1}$ There is no significant difference in Autonomy between male and female leaders as perceived by leaders.

$H_{011.2}$ There is no significant difference in Autonomy between male and female leaders as perceived by subordinates.

$H_{012.1}$ There is no significant difference in Nurturing style between male and female leaders as perceived by leaders.

$H_{012.2}$ There is no significant difference in Nurturing style between male and female leaders as perceived by subordinates.

$H_{013.1}$: There is no significant difference in Organizational commitment between male and female leaders as perceived by leaders.

$H_{013.2}$: There is no significant difference in Organizational commitment between male and female leaders as perceived by subordinates.

$H_{014.1}$: There is no significant difference in extent of Optimism between male and female leaders as perceived by leaders.

$H_{014.2}$: There is no significant difference in extent of Optimism between male and female leaders as perceived by subordinates.

$H_{015.1}$: There is no significant difference in Performance-oriented approach between male and female leaders as perceived by leaders.

$H_{015.2}$: There is no significant difference in Performance-oriented approach between male and female leaders as perceived by subordinates.

$H_{016.1}$: There is no significant difference in Assertiveness style between male and female leaders as perceived by leaders.

$H_{016.2}$: There is no significant difference in Assertiveness style between male and female leaders as perceived by subordinates.

$H_{017.}$: There is no significant difference in transformational leadership approach between Private and Public Organizational leaders as perceived by them.

$H_{018}$: There is no significant difference in transformational leadership approach between private and public sector leaders as perceived by subordinates.

$H_{019.1}$: There is no significant difference in open communication approach between private and public organizational leaders as perceived by leaders.

$H_{019.2}$: There is no significant difference in open communication approach between private and public organizational leaders as perceived by subordinates.

$H_{020.1}$: There is no significant difference in Delegation style between Private and Public Organizational leaders as perceived by leaders.

$H_{020.2}$: There is no significant difference in Delegation style between Private and Public Organizational leaders as perceived by subordinates.

$H_{021.1}$: There is no significant difference in Conviction between Private and Public Organizational as perceived by leaders.

$H_{021.2}$: There is no significant difference in Conviction between Private and Public Organizational leaders as perceived by subordinates.

$H_{022.1}$: There is no significant difference in Team working spirit between Private and Public Organizational leaders as perceived by leaders.

$H_{022.2}$: There is no significant difference in Team working spirit between Private and Public Organizational leaders as perceived by subordinates.

$H_{023.1}$: There is no significant difference in Decision making skills between Private and Public Organizational leaders as perceived by leaders.

$H_{023.2}$: There is no significant difference in Decision making skills between Private and Public Organizational leaders as perceived by subordinates.

$H_{024.1.}$: There is no significant difference in Attitude towards risk taking between Private and Public Organizational leaders as perceived by leaders.

$H_{024.2.}$: There is no significant difference in Attitude towards risk taking between Private and Public Organizational leaders as perceived by subordinates.

$H_{025.1.}$: There is no significant difference in conflict management approach between private and public organizational leaders as perceived by leaders

$H_{025.2.}$: There is no significant difference in conflict management approach between private and public organizational leaders as perceived by subordinates.

$H_{026.1.}$: There is no significant difference in People development style between Private and Public Organizational leaders as perceived by leaders.

$H_{026.2.}$: There is no significant difference in People development style between Private and Public Organizational leaders as perceived by subordinates.

$H_{027.1.}$: There is no significant difference in Autonomy between Private and Public Organizational as perceived by leaders.

$H_{027.2.}$: There is no significant difference in Autonomy between Private and Public Organizational leaders as perceived by subordinates.

$H_{028.1.}$: There is no significant difference in Nurturing style between Private and Public Organizational as perceived by leaders.

$H_{028.2.}$: There is no significant difference in Nurturing style between Private and Public Organizational as perceived by subordinates.

$H_{029.1.}$: There is no significant difference in Organizational commitment between Private and Public Organizational leaders as perceived by leaders.

$H_{029.2}$: There is no significant difference in Organizational commitment between Private and Public Organizational leaders as perceived by subordinates.

$H_{030.1}$: There is no significant difference in extent of Optimism between Private and Public Organizational leaders as perceived by leaders.

$H_{030.2}$: There is no significant difference in extent of Optimism between Private and Public Organizational leaders as perceived by subordinates.

$H_{031.1}$: There is no significant difference in Performance-oriented approach between private and public organizational leaders as perceived by leaders

$H_{031.2}$: There is no significant difference in performance-oriented approach between private and public organizational leaders as perceived by subordinates.

$H_{032.1}$: There is no significant difference in Assertiveness style between Private and Public Organizational leaders as perceived by leaders.

$H_{032.2}$: There is no significant difference in Assertiveness style between Private and Public Organizational leaders as perceived by subordinates.

## 3.6 SCOPE OF STUDY

The following details describe the scope of study:

1. Male and Female of Private and Public Sectors were included for the purpose of study.
2. Demographic variables like- age, gender, marital status, income, education, occupation Experience, designation etc. were considered.
3. The study has been conducted on the transformational style of leadership.

## 3.7 THE UNIVERSE AND SAMPLE SIZE

The universe included the male and females of private and public sectors those who were leaders and follow the transformational style of leadership and also the subordinates working under their supervision and guidance at State level (M.P.). In the public and private sectors, the following were included such as; IT, Healthcare Hospitality, Academics, Banking & Insurance and Manufacturing.

The sampling method applied was non-probability judgement sampling method, also known as purposive sampling. In this sampling, the researcher picks a sample from the population, which he/she considers a representative of the population. All elements of the population are not having equal opportunity to get included in the sample. Judgement of the researcher becomes major factor.

Primary data were collected from employees working in private and public sector companies. Total 100 male leaders and 100 female leaders and in the same way 100 male subordinates and 100 female subordinates were the sample size to be selected purposively. In all total 400 respondents were chosen for this study. They were asked to fill the questionnaire regarding the leadership styles of male and female leaders. The population were from Madhya Pradesh. It is expected that this study would prove to be a significant input towards highlighting transformational leadership style in female and male leaders.

There was no equal representation of respondents in terms of demographic variables. However, gender, age, marital status, qualification, designation, profession, experience and income had a major role in data analysis.

**3.8 DATA SOURCES:**

Before starting the research, primary and secondary data are always collected. Secondary data are also known as historical data, which are earlier collected by prior researchers across the world. This data is of great significance in research since it forms the foundation of primary data. In the research, secondary data were collected from sources like- textbooks, journals, business magazines, newspapers, Internet, brochures etc.

Primary data is first-hand data collected freshly by the researcher. For the purpose of collecting primary data, questionnaire is a common instrument for researchers. A questionnaire consists of a set of questions (open-ended as well as closed-ended) for the purpose of collecting data from the respondents. Questionnaires are more often used in case the data are to be collected from a large population about their variables like: awareness, perception, expectations, taste & preferences, effectiveness and behaviour.

Administering the questionnaire for collecting data can be done in many ways. It can either be administered personally; or through mailer, email or telephonically. A questionnaire may be structured or unstructured depending on the need of the researcher. In structured questionnaire, the questions and probable responses are visibly pre-specified; in non-structured questionnaire, the questions are kept flexible and the respondents are allowed to use flexibility to answer the questions in their own way.

Similarly, the response pattern of respondents may differ in terms of open-ended and close-ended questions. Open-ended questions are time consuming; but respondents give detailed opinions about the suggestions; problems which are not shown in closed-ended questions. Close-ended questionnaire has the pre-specified alternatives and the respondents are supposed to choose any one from among the specified alternatives. In this study, it was a self-administered questionnaire that consisted of the closed-ended questions. It facilitated the respondents in filling their opinion about the topic. There was no ambiguity in any portion of the questionnaire. The questionnaire was tested by using pilot study on 30 respondents. After making minor changes, it was finalized for study.

### 3.8.1 STRUCTURE OF THE QUESTIONNAIRE

For this study two separate questionnaires were framed one for the leaders and the other one for the subordinates. The first part of questionnaire on leaders contained important information about the responses in terms of gender, age, marital status, qualification, profession, sectors, years of experience, experience in current organization, designation, income, etc. This section was highly useful in getting vital information about the demography of respondents. The main part was divided into four parameters where first parameter was pertaining to individualized consideration in which the questions were laid on open communication, delegation and conviction in self, the second parameter was on intellectual stimulation and the statements were on teamwork, decision making skills, attitude to risk taking, conflict management, developing people, autonomy and nurturing, the third parameter was on inspirational motivation and the statements were included organizational commitment and optimism and the last parameter was on idealized influence and the question on assertiveness, performance oriented, where respondents were asked to rank from among the options ranging from strongly agree, agree, neutral, disagree and strongly disagree. On the same pattern the next questionnaire was prepared for the subordinates and the respondents were asked the questions on the same parameters, how they perceive the transformational style of their leaders.

## 3.9 ANALYSIS OF DATA

Data analysis process involves applying the reasoning to analyze and interpret the primary data collected by the researcher. The choice of analytical technique/s depends on the characteristics of research design and hypothesis. The collected data from respondents were important because it contained all the relevant information needed to fulfil the objectives of research. Before applying statistical techniques for data analysis, the data collected was tabulated to facilitate interpretation process.

The primary collected data was converted into a user-friendly format by coding. Using MS Excel, data transformation was done in spreadsheet, where the response of all respondents against relevant questions was entered. It was arranged in a tabular manner in rows and columns, where rows represented respondents and the columns indicated relevant questions/statements against which the response was recorded. Finally, a rectangular data matrix was formed on spreadsheet.

## 3.9.1 STATISTICAL TOOLS FOR ANALYSIS

The selection of statistical technique gives suitable directions for data interpretation and further implications. The correct technique gives significant suggestions for the probable findings. After tabulation, data analysis was performed by using SPSS 20.0 (Statistical Package for Social Science). Descriptive statistics used in this study included mean, frequencies and standard deviations. With the help of SPSS, analysis was done and hypothesis testing was done accordingly.

Statistical techniques used in this study were t-test for all the hypotheses.

**T-test:** For applying *t*-test, we work out the value of test statistic (i.e., '*t*') and then compare with the table value of *t* (based on '*t*' distribution) at certain level of significance for given degrees of freedom (i.e. .05). If the calculated value of '*t*' is either equal to or exceeds the table value, we infer that the difference is significant, but if calculated value of *t* is less than the concerning table value of *t*, the difference is not treated as significant. The independent sample t test shows two tests i.e. Levene's test & T test. Levene's test is for equality of variances. If the significance values are less than .05, so variances are assumed to be equal.

By applying the statistical techniques, data analysis and interpretation process was carried out thoroughly and comprehensive results were determined. Due to appropriate selection of statistical tools, the results were validated and justified. These results are translated into user-friendly manner from the statistical data and are explained with the help of tables. The interpretation of the data has given useful insights into the subject matter, which are valuable for leaders and subordinates at large. Each aspect of the subject matter has been derived in the results section. Detailed results of data analysis along with their interpretations have been mentioned in forthcoming chapter.

## 3.10: DEMOGRAPHIC PROFILE OF LEADERS

For the analysis total 200 leaders were chosen among them 100 were males and 100 were females from different sectors. They were from both public and private organizations. They were on various designations such as; Head of the Departments, Regional and Branch Managers, Directors/Professors, Medical Professionals etc.

|       |           | Frequency | Percent | Valid Percent | Cumulative Percent |
|-------|-----------|-----------|---------|---------------|--------------------|
|       | MARRIED   | 119       | 59.5    | 59.5          | 59.5               |
| Valid | UNMARRIED | 81        | 40.5    | 40.5          | 100.0              |
|       | Total     | 200       | 100.0   | 100.0         |                    |

## TABLE 3.1: ON MARITAL STATUS OF LEADERS

From the above data shows on marital status of the leaders, it is revealed that out of 200 leaders, 59.5% were married and rest 40.5% were unmarried. Married leaders have more maturity in taking decisions and also experienced in reflecting behaviour in given situations

|       |       | Frequency | Percent | Valid Percent | Cumulative Percent |
|-------|-------|-----------|---------|---------------|--------------------|
|       | YES   | 176       | 88.0    | 88.0          | 88.0               |
| Valid | NO    | 24        | 12.0    | 12.0          | 100.0              |
|       | Total | 200       | 100.0   | 100.0         |                    |

## TABLE 3.2: ON PROMOTERS OF ORGANIZATIONS (LEADERS )

The leaders were asked on the question of promoters of organization, 88% agreed and 12% disagreed as those who said No they were not the promoters of their organizations, they do their job only just to earn their livelihood and nothing else. These leaders are not concerned with any future vision for the growth and development.

|  |  | Frequency | Percent | Valid Percent | Cumulative Percent |
|---|---|---|---|---|---|
| Valid | HEALTHCARE | 82 | 41.0 | 41.0 | 41.0 |
|  | HOSPITALITY | 37 | 18.5 | 18.5 | 59.5 |
|  | BANKING & INSURANCE | 14 | 7.0 | 7.0 | 66.5 |
|  | IT | 12 | 6.0 | 6.0 | 72.5 |
|  | ACADEMICS | 14 | 7.0 | 7.0 | 79.5 |
|  | MANUFACTURING | 41 | 20.5 | 20.5 | 100.0 |
|  | Total | 200 | 100.0 | 100.0 |  |

## TABLE 3.3: ON SECTOR OF LEADERS

Out of 200 leaders, 41 per cent was in healthcare industry, 18.5 per cent in hospitality sector, 7 per cent was in banking & insurance sector, 6 per cent in IT sector, 7 per cent in Academics and remaining 20.5% in manufacturing units. The above data reveals that the majority of leaders were chosen from the healthcare industry which is very demanding in the service organizations. But on the other hand the less per cent was from IT as these leaders do not have time to fill the questionnaires.

|  |  | Frequency | Percent | Valid Percent | Cumulative Percent |
|---|---|---|---|---|---|
| Valid | GRADUATE | 50 | 25.0 | 25.0 | 25.0 |
|  | PG | 135 | 67.5 | 67.5 | 92.5 |
|  | PH.D & OTHERS | 15 | 7.5 | 7.5 | 100.0 |
|  | Total | 200 | 100.0 | 100.0 |  |

## TABLE 3.4: ON EDUCATION OF LEADERS

The table reveals that 25 per cent leaders were Graduates, 67.5 per cent were Post Graduates and rest 7.5

per cent were Ph.D and others Degrees in various disciplines. PGs are enough mature to feel the attributes of leadership and also capable enough to apply the styles of leadership in different situations.

| | | Frequency | Percent | Valid Percent | Cumulative Percent |
|---|---|---|---|---|---|
| | UPTO10 YEARS | 109 | 54.5 | 54.5 | 54.5 |
| | 10-20 YEARS | 56 | 28.0 | 28.0 | 82.5 |
| Valid | 20-30 YEARS | 15 | 7.5 | 7.5 | 90.0 |
| | >30 YEARS | 20 | 10.0 | 10.0 | 100.0 |
| | Total | 200 | 100.0 | 100.0 | |

## TABLE 3.5: ON EXPERIENCE OF LEADERS

Regarding the total experience of Leaders, 54.5 per cent have below 10 years of experience, 28 per cent have 10-20 years of experience, 7.5 per cent have 20-30 years of experience and 10 per cent have more than 30 years of experience. 10 years of experience is enough to examine the judgmental capabilities of any Leader.

| | | Frequency | Percent | Valid Percent | Cumulative Percent |
|---|---|---|---|---|---|
| | <35 YEARS | 104 | 52.0 | 52.0 | 52.0 |
| | 35-45 YEARS | 56 | 28.0 | 28.0 | 80.0 |
| Valid | 45-55 YEARS | 27 | 13.5 | 13.5 | 93.5 |
| | >55 YEARS | 13 | 6.5 | 6.5 | 100.0 |
| | Total | 200 | 100.0 | 100.0 | |

## TABLE 3.6: ON AGE GROUP OF LEADERS

Form the data analysis on age group shows that 52 per cent leaders were under 35 years of age group, 28 per cent were between 35-45 age group, 13.5 per cent between 45-55 age group and rest 6.5 per cent were more than 55 years of age group. The majority of the leaders' age group was below 35 years. This age is known as the mature age and the person has more mature rational faculty and intellectual competency.

| | Frequency | Percent | Valid Percent | Cumulative Percent |
|---|---|---|---|---|
| UPTO 5 LAC | 63 | 31.5 | 31.5 | 31.5 |
| 5-10 LACS | 70 | 35.0 | 35.0 | 66.5 |
| Valid   10-20 LACS | 42 | 21.0 | 21.0 | 87.5 |
| >20 LACS | 25 | 12.5 | 12.5 | 100.0 |
| Total | 200 | 100.0 | 100.0 | |

## TABLE 3.7: ON INCOME GROUP OF LEADERS

Regarding the income level, the data reveals that 31.5 per cent have less than 5 lac as an annual income, 35 per cent have 5-1- lacs as an annual income, 21 per cent have 10-20 lacs as an annual income and remaining 12.5 per cent have more than 20 lac as an annual income.

| | Frequency | Percent | Valid Percent | Cumulative Percent |
|---|---|---|---|---|
| MARRIED | 131 | 65.5 | 65.5 | 65.5 |
| Valid   UNMARRIED | 69 | 34.5 | 34.5 | 100.0 |
| Total | 200 | 100.0 | 100.0 | |

## TABLE 3.8: ON MARITAL STATUS OF SUBORDINATES

From the above data shows on marital status of the leaders, it is revealed that out of 200 subordinates, 65.5% were married and rest 34.5% were unmarried. Married subordinates have more maturity in taking decisions and also experienced in reflecting behaviour in given situations.

| | | Frequency | Percent | Valid Percent | Cumulative Percent |
|---|---|---|---|---|---|
| | YES | 168 | 84.0 | 84.0 | 84.0 |
| Valid | NO | 32 | 16.0 | 16.0 | 100.0 |
| | Total | 200 | 100.0 | 100.0 | |

## TABLE 3.9: ON PROMOTERS OF SUBORDINATES

The subordinates were asked on the question of promoters of organization, 84% agreed and 16% disagreed as those who said No they were not the promoters of their organizations, they do their job only just to earn their livelihood and nothing else. These subordinates are not concerned with any future vision for the growth and development.

| | | Frequency | Percent | Valid Percent | Cumulative Percent |
|---|---|---|---|---|---|
| | HEALTHCARE | 73 | 36.5 | 36.5 | 36.5 |
| | HOSPITALITY | 46 | 23.0 | 23.0 | 59.5 |
| | BANKING & INSURANCE | 22 | 11.0 | 11.0 | 70.5 |
| Valid | IT | 4 | 2.0 | 2.0 | 72.5 |
| | ACADEMICS | 20 | 10.0 | 10.0 | 82.5 |
| | MANUFACTURING | 35 | 17.5 | 17.5 | 100.0 |
| | Total | 200 | 100.0 | 100.0 | |

## TABLE 3.10: ON SECTORS OF SUBORDINATES

Out of 200 subordinates, 36.5 percent was in healthcare industry, 23 per cent in hospitality sector, 11 per cent was in banking & insurance sector, 2 per cent in IT sector, 10 per cent in Academics and remaining 17.5% in manufacturing units. The above data reveals that the majority of subordinates were chosen from the healthcare industry which is very demanding in the service organizations. But on the other hand the less percent was from IT as these subordinates do not have time to fill the questionnaires.

|  |  | Frequency | Percent | Valid Percent | Cumulative Percent |
|---|---|---|---|---|---|
|  | GRADUATE | 84 | 42.0 | 42.0 | 42.0 |
|  | PG | 108 | 54.0 | 54.0 | 96.0 |
| Valid | PH.D & OTHERS | 8 | 4.0 | 4.0 | 100.0 |
|  | Total | 200 | 100.0 | 100.0 |  |

## TABLE 3.11: ON EDUCATION OF SUBORDINATES

The table reveals that 42 per cent subordinates were Graduates, 54 per cent were Post Graduates and rest 4 percent were Ph.D and others Degrees in various disciplines. PGs are enough mature to feel the attributes of leadership and also capable enough to follow their leaders in different situations.

|  |  | Frequency | Percent | Valid Percent | Cumulative Percent |
|---|---|---|---|---|---|
|  | UPTO 5 YEARS | 120 | 60.0 | 60.0 | 60.0 |
|  | 5-10 YEARS | 45 | 22.5 | 22.5 | 82.5 |
| Valid | 10-15 YEARS | 25 | 12.5 | 12.5 | 95.0 |
|  | >15 YEARS | 10 | 5.0 | 5.0 | 100.0 |
|  | Total | 200 | 100.0 | 100.0 |  |

## TABLE 3.12: ON TOTAL EXPERIENCE OF SUBORDINATES

Regarding the total experience of subordinates, 60 per cent have below 5 years of experience, 22.5 per cent have 5-10 years of experience, 12.5 per cent have 10-15 years of experience and 5 per cent have more than 15 years of experience. Max. 15 years of experience is enough to examine the capabilities to follow their Leaders.

|  |  | Frequency | Percent | Valid Percent | Cumulative Percent |
|---|---|---|---|---|---|
|  | <25 YEARS | 119 | 59.5 | 59.5 | 59.5 |
|  | 25-35 YEARS | 51 | 25.5 | 25.5 | 85.0 |
| Valid | 35-40 YEARS | 24 | 12.0 | 12.0 | 97.0 |
|  | >40 YEARS | 6 | 3.0 | 3.0 | 100.0 |
|  | Total | 200 | 100.0 | 100.0 |  |

## TABLE 3.13: ON AGE GROUP OF SUBORDINATES

Form the data analysis on age group shows that 59.5 per cent subordinates were under 25 years of age group, 29.5 per cent were between 25-35 age group, 12 per cent between 35-40 age group and rest 3 per cent were more than 40 years of age group. The majority of the subordinates' age group was below 35 years. This age is known as the mature age and the person has more mature rational faculty and intellectual competency.

|  |  | Frequency | Percent | Valid Percent | Cumulative Percent |
|---|---|---|---|---|---|
| Valid | UPTO 2 LAC | 73 | 36.5 | 36.5 | 36.5 |
|  | 2-5 LAC | 60 | 30.0 | 30.0 | 66.5 |
|  | 5-10 LAC | 53 | 26.5 | 26.5 | 93.0 |
|  | >10 LAC | 14 | 7.0 | 7.0 | 100.0 |
|  | Total | 200 | 100.0 | 100.0 |  |

## TABLE 3.14: ON INCOME GROUP OF SUBORDINATES

Regarding the income level, the data reveals that 36.5 per cent have less than 2 lac as an annual income, 30 per cent have 2-5 lacs as an annual income, 26.5 per cent have 5-10 lacs as an annual income and remaining 7 per cent have more than 10 lac as an annual income.

|  |  | Frequency | Percent | Valid Percent | Cumulative Percent |
|---|---|---|---|---|---|
| Valid | <1 YEAR | 53 | 26.5 | 26.5 | 26.5 |
|  | 1-5 YEARS | 54 | 27.0 | 27.0 | 53.5 |
|  | 5-10 YEARS | 76 | 38.0 | 38.0 | 91.5 |
|  | >10 YEARS | 17 | 8.5 | 8.5 | 100.0 |
|  | Total | 200 | 100.0 | 100.0 |  |

## TABLE 3.15: ON CURRENT EXPERIENCE IN ORGANIZATION OF SUBORDINATES

Regarding the current experience in the present organizations of subordinates, 26.5 per cent have below 1 year of experience, 27 per cent have 1-5 years of experience, 38 per cent have 5-10 years of experience and 8.5 per cent have more than 10 years of experience. Max. 10 years of current experience in present organization is enough to examine the capabilities of the subordinates.

| | | Frequency | Percent | Valid Percent | Cumulative Percent |
|---|---|---|---|---|---|
| Valid | MALE | 168 | 84.0 | 84.0 | 84.0 |
| | FEMALE | 32 | 16.0 | 16.0 | 100.0 |
| | Total | 200 | 100.0 | 100.0 | |

## TABLE 3.16: ON GENDER OF SUBORDINATES' LEADERS

Out of 200 subordinates 84 per cent responded that they have male leaders and rest 16 percent said that they have female leaders. The ratio of female leaders is very low but now the women are also marching ahead in all the areas.

# IV
# DATA ANALYSIS AND FINDINGS

## 4.1 INTRODUCTION:

Research is a process of exploring new areas of existing concepts, phenomenon or ideology. With clear objectives and hypothesis, research in social science gets proper shape. Analysis of the data collected from primary or secondary sources paves the way for the results. This study has included secondary data as a reference; but primary data has been the major source of analysis. With proper selection of hypothesis and data analysis techniques, the data was tabulated and analyzed. This chapter talks about the hypothesis related to transformational leadership approach between male and female leaders as perceived by them and their subordinates. Further, this study tries to explore the difference in various approaches between male and female leaders. The data was collected from the leaders as well as the members under him or her in selected organizations. Such approaches include broad categories like individualized consideration; intellectual stimulation; inspirational motivation and idealized influence. Significant difference between male & female leaders in terms of different transformational leadership approach is been measured.

**4.1.1 Summary of Hypothesis Testing:** Before applying the statistical test, Primary data were collected from employees working in private and public sector companies. Total 100 male leaders and 100 female leaders and in the same way 100 male subordinates and 100 female subordinates were the sample size to be selected purposively. In all total 400 respondents were chosen for this study from among public and private sector. For testing the hypothesis through t-test, it was found that out of 16 hypotheses two hypotheses namely $H_{08}$ and $H_{16}$ were rejected and rest were accepted. It can be inferred that when it comes to transformational leadership, significant differences were found among male and female leaders with respect to attitude towards risk taking and assertiveness style. However, among other parameters like-open communication, delegation style, conviction, team working spirit, decision making skills, conflict management, people development style, autonomy, nurturing style, organizational commitment, extent of optimism and performance-oriented approach, no significant differences were found in male and female leaders. Similarly, there was no significant difference found in transformational leadership approach between male and female leaders as perceived by them and also as perceived by their subordinates. While most of the factors were found same in terms of transformational leadership approach except two, it can be inferred at large that male and female leaders are same in most of the characteristics. As a results,

Half of the Sub-hypotheses were accepted and half are rejected.

## 4.2 DETAILED DATA ANALYSIS RESULTS:

The comprehensive representation of the results and their interpretation is shown in the following section:

**$H_1$: There is no significant difference in transformational leadership approach between male and female leaders as perceived by them.**

From the below analysis of hypothesis where we have analyzed significant difference between different transformational leadership approach between male & female leaders as perceived by them, we can observe that out of 16 hypothesis, 14 stands accepted and 2 are rejected with respect to attitude towards risk & assertiveness style. As majority of the hypothesis are accepted, so we can conclude that there is no significant difference in transformational leadership approach between male and female leaders as perceived by them.

**$H_2$: There is no significant difference in transformational leadership approach between male and female leaders as perceived by their subordinates.**

From the below hypothesis testing, where we have analyzed significant difference between different transformational leadership approach between male & female leaders as perceived by subordinates, it was found that out of 16 hypotheses two hypotheses namely $H_{08}$ and $H_{16}$ were rejected and rest were accepted. It can be inferred that when it comes to transformational leadership, significant differences were found among male and female leaders with respect to attitude towards risk taking and assertiveness style. As majority of the hypothesis are accepted, so we can conclude that there is no significant difference in transformational leadership approach between male and female leaders as perceived by subordinates.

**H$_{3.1}$: There is no significant difference in Open communication approach between male and female leaders as perceived by leaders.**

|  | Gender | N | Mean | Std. Deviation | Std. Error Mean |
|---|---|---|---|---|---|
| Open_Commu_Policies | Male | 100 | 4.08 | 1.032 | .103 |
|  | Female | 100 | 3.88 | 1.131 | .113 |
| free_frank_ Commu | Male | 100 | 3.87 | 1.169 | .117 |
|  | Female | 100 | 3.81 | 1.134 | .113 |
| Open_door_Policy | Male | 100 | 3.84 | 1.012 | .101 |
|  | Female | 100 | 3.80 | 1.025 | .102 |
| Honest_Answer | Male | 100 | 3.56 | 1.175 | .117 |
|  | Female | 100 | 3.45 | 1.192 | .119 |

**Table No. 4.1: Group Statistics for Open Communication approach between male & female leaders as perceived by leaders.**

The table talks about descriptive statistics which shows the values of mean & standard deviation. The transformational leaders have shown their agreement for open communication approach in all the attributes irrespective of their gender.

| | | Levene's Test for Equality of Variances | | t-test for Equality of Means | | | | | | | |
|---|---|---|---|---|---|---|---|---|---|---|---|
| | | F | Sig. | T | df | Sig. (2-tailed) | Mean Difference | Std. Error Difference | 95% Confidence Interval of the Difference | | |
| | | | | | | | | | Lower | Upper | |
| Open_ Commu_ Policies | Equal variances assumed | 1.468 | .227 | 1.307 | 198 | .193 | .200 | .153 | -.102 | .502 | |
| | Equal variances not assumed | | | 1.307 | 196.359 | .193 | .200 | .153 | -.102 | .502 | |
| free_frank _Commu | Equal variances assumed | .001 | .971 | .368 | 198 | .713 | .060 | .163 | -.261 | .381 | |
| | Equal variances not assumed | | | .368 | 197.820 | .713 | .060 | .163 | -.261 | .381 | |
| Open_doo r_Policy | Equal variances assumed | .105 | .747 | .278 | 198 | .782 | .040 | .144 | -.244 | .324 | |
| | Equal variances not assumed | | | .278 | 197.969 | .782 | .040 | .144 | -.244 | .324 | |
| Honest_ Answer | Equal variances assumed | .181 | .671 | .657 | 198 | .512 | .110 | .167 | -.220 | .440 | |
| | Equal variances not assumed | | | .657 | 197.957 | .512 | .110 | .167 | -.220 | .440 | |

## Table No. 4.2: Independent Samples Test for Open Communication approach between male & female leaders as perceived by leaders

To see the result of Independent Sample t test, first we have to look for the "Levene's Test for Equality of Variance" section. The p value for variance is 0.227, 0.971, 0.747 & 0.671 all are higher than .05, therefore for t test we have assumed equal variance & we will look at the top row for t test result. The p values for t test are 0.193, 0.713, 0.782 and 0.512 which indicates that there is no significant difference in Open communication approach between male and female leaders as perceived by leaders. Hence the hypothesis stands accepted.

**H$_{3.2}$: There is no significant difference in Open communication approach between male and female leaders as perceived by subordinates.**

|  | Gender | N | Mean | Std. Deviation | Std. Error Mean |
|---|---|---|---|---|---|
| Open_Commu_Policies | Male | 100 | 3.99 | 1.150 | .115 |
|  | Female | 100 | 3.85 | 1.140 | .114 |
| free_frank_Commu | Male | 100 | 3.79 | 1.166 | .117 |
|  | Female | 100 | 3.70 | 1.219 | .122 |
| Open_door_Policy | Male | 100 | 3.63 | 1.134 | .113 |
|  | Female | 100 | 3.51 | 1.322 | .132 |
| Honest_Answer | Male | 100 | 3.51 | 1.168 | .117 |
|  | Female | 100 | 3.28 | 1.248 | .125 |

**Table No. 4.3: Group Statistics for Open Communication approach between male & female leaders as perceived by Subordinates.**

The above table talks about the mean values of different attributes of Open Communication Approach between male & female leaders as perceived by their subordinates. The mean value in case of "Open door policy is encouraged by my leader for communication, My questions are being answered openly and honestly" is close to 3 which indicates their neutral opinion while in other attributes like "Policies and procedures are explained to me well by my leader/ supervisor, My leader encourages free and frank communication at various levels" the mean value is close to 4 which shows agreement of leaders for the above factors irrespective of their gender.

| | | Levene's Test for Equality of Variances | | t-test for Equality of Means | | | | | | | |
|---|---|---|---|---|---|---|---|---|---|---|---|
| | | F | Sig. | T | df | Sig. (2-tailed) | Mean Difference | Std. Error Difference | 95% Confidence Interval of the Difference | | |
| | | | | | | | | | Lower | Upper |
| Open_ Commu_ Policies | Equal variances assumed | .567 | .452 | .864 | 198 | .388 | .140 | .162 | -.179 | .459 |
| | Equal variances not assumed | | | .864 | 197.985 | .388 | .140 | .162 | -.179 | .459 |
| free_frank _Commu | Equal variances assumed | .673 | .413 | .534 | 198 | .594 | .090 | .169 | -.243 | .423 |
| | Equal variances not assumed | | | .534 | 197.616 | .594 | .090 | .169 | -.243 | .423 |
| Open_ door_Poli cy | Equal variances assumed | 3.124 | .079 | .689 | 198 | .492 | .120 | .174 | -.223 | .463 |
| | Equal variances not assumed | | | .689 | 193.522 | .492 | .120 | .174 | -.224 | .464 |
| Honest_ Answer | Equal variances assumed | 1.271 | .261 | 1.346 | 198 | .180 | .230 | .171 | -.107 | .567 |
| | Equal variances not assumed | | | 1.346 | 197.134 | .180 | .230 | .171 | -.107 | .567 |

**Table No. 4.4: Independent Samples Test for Open Communication approach between male & female leaders as perceived by Subordinates**

The Independent Sample t test shows two test i.e. Levene's test for equality of variances & t test. In Levene's test if the p value is less than .05, equal variance are not assumed. In all the cases the p value>0.05, so variances are assumed equal. For t test result we have to look at the top row, respective significance values are 0.388, 0.594, 0.492 and 0.180 which are higher than .05 which means there is no significant difference in Open communication approach between male and female leaders as perceived by subordinates. Hence the hypothesis is accepted.

**H$_{4.1}$: There is no significant difference in Delegation style between male and female leaders as perceived by leaders**

|  | Gender | N | Mean | Std. Deviation | Std. Error Mean |
|---|---|---|---|---|---|
| Rare_Delegation | Male | 100 | 3.94 | 1.127 | .113 |
|  | Female | 100 | 3.81 | 1.212 | .121 |
| Regular_Delegation | Male | 100 | 3.67 | 1.083 | .108 |
|  | Female | 100 | 3.57 | 1.085 | .108 |
| Positive_ Negative_Consid | Male | 100 | 3.90 | .905 | .090 |
|  | Female | 100 | 3.83 | .943 | .094 |
| Close_Supervision | Male | 100 | 3.95 | 1.104 | .110 |
|  | Female | 100 | 3.75 | 1.132 | .113 |

## Table No. 4.5: Group Statistics for Delegation style between male & female leaders as perceived by leaders.

The table talks about the group statistics of one of the attribute of transformational leadership called Delegation Style on the basis of gender as perceived by leaders. The mean value of male and female seems to be same which shows their similar opinion for Delegation Style. The values of standard deviation are also very less which shows low degree of variation in their responses.

| | | Levene's Test for Equality of Variances | | t-test for Equality of Means | | | | | | | |
| --- | --- | --- | --- | --- | --- | --- | --- | --- | --- | --- |
| | | F | Sig. | T | df | Sig. (2-tailed) | Mean Difference | Std. Error Difference | 95% Confidence Interval of the Difference | |
| | | | | | | | | | Lower | Upper |
| Rare_ Delegation | Equal variances assumed | 1.683 | .196 | .786 | 198 | .433 | .130 | .165 | -.196 | .456 |
| | Equal variances not assumed | | | .786 | 196.954 | .433 | .130 | .165 | -.196 | .456 |
| Regular_ Delegation | Equal variances assumed | .008 | .929 | .652 | 198 | .515 | .100 | .153 | -.202 | .402 |
| | Equal variances not assumed | | | .652 | 197.999 | .515 | .100 | .153 | -.202 | .402 |
| Positive_ Negative_ Consid | Equal variances assumed | .381 | .538 | .536 | 198 | .593 | .070 | .131 | -.188 | .328 |
| | Equal variances not assumed | | | .536 | 197.651 | .593 | .070 | .131 | -.188 | .328 |
| Close_ Supervision | Equal variances assumed | .981 | .323 | 1.265 | 198 | .207 | .200 | .158 | -.112 | .512 |
| | Equal variances not assumed | | | 1.265 | 197.884 | .207 | .200 | .158 | -.112 | .512 |

## Table No. 4.6: Independent Samples Test for Delegation style between male & female leaders as perceived by leaders

The p value in levene's test of equality is higher than 0.05 in all the cases. So, we will look at equal variances assumed i.e. top row for t test result. All the p value of t test> 0.05 this indicates that there is no significant difference in Delegation style between male and female leaders as perceived by leaders. Hence the hypothesis is accepted

$H_{4.2}$: **There is no significant difference in Delegation style between male and female leaders as perceived by**

**subordinates.**

|  | Gender | N | Mean | Std. Deviation | Std. Error Mean |
|---|---|---|---|---|---|
| Rare_Delegation | Male | 100 | 3.75 | 1.192 | .119 |
|  | Female | 100 | 3.71 | 1.297 | .130 |
| Regular_Delegation | Male | 100 | 3.57 | 1.121 | .112 |
|  | Female | 100 | 3.41 | 1.181 | .118 |
| Positive_Negative_Consid | Male | 100 | 3.80 | .943 | .094 |
|  | Female | 100 | 3.54 | 1.141 | .114 |
| Close_Supervision | Male | 100 | 3.82 | 1.201 | .120 |
|  | Female | 100 | 3.61 | 1.262 | .126 |

**Table No. 4.7: Group Statistics for Delegation style between male & female leaders as perceived by Subordinates.**

The Group Statistics table shows the mean & standard deviation of different attribute of Delegation Style on the basis of gender as perceived by their subordinates. We can observe form the above table that the mean value of males & females are almost same which indicates male & female leaders are same in terms of transformational delegation style.

| | | Levene's Test for Equality of Variances | | t-test for Equality of Means | | | | | | | |
|---|---|---|---|---|---|---|---|---|---|---|---|
| | | F | Sig. | t | Df | Sig. (2-tailed) | Mean Difference | Std. Error Difference | 95% Confidence Interval of the Difference | | |
| | | | | | | | | | Lower | Upper |
| Rare_ Delegation | Equal variances assumed | 1.156 | .284 | .227 | 198 | .821 | .040 | .176 | -.307 | .387 |
| | Equal variances not assumed | | | .227 | 196.610 | .821 | .040 | .176 | -.307 | .387 |
| Regular_ Delegation | Equal variances assumed | .106 | .745 | .982 | 198 | .327 | .160 | .163 | -.161 | .481 |
| | Equal variances not assumed | | | .982 | 197.465 | .327 | .160 | .163 | -.161 | .481 |
| Positive_ Negative_ Consid | Equal variances assumed | 5.389 | .021 | 1.757 | 198 | .080 | .260 | .148 | -.032 | .552 |
| | Equal variances not assumed | | | 1.757 | 191.217 | .081 | .260 | .148 | -.032 | .552 |
| Close_ Supervision | Equal variances assumed | .933 | .335 | 1.205 | 198 | .230 | .210 | .174 | -.134 | .554 |
| | Equal variances not assumed | | | 1.205 | 197.506 | .230 | .210 | .174 | -.134 | .554 |

## Table No. 4.8: Independent Samples Test for Delegation style between male & female leaders as perceived by Subordinates

For looking at the result of t test, first we have to assume for the equal variances with the help of levene's test for equality of variances. The p values of levene's test are higher than 0.05 except in attribute called "Positive as well as negative aspects are considered by the leader before taking any action" where we will assume unequal variance and in all other cases equal variances will be considered. So the respective t test p values are .821, .327, 0.081 & 0.230 which means there is no significant difference in Delegation style between male and female leaders as perceived by subordinates. Hence the hypothesis stands accepted.

$H_{5.1}$: **There is no significant difference in Conviction between male and female leaders as perceived by leaders.**

|  | Gender | N | Mean | Std. Deviation | Std. Error Mean |
|---|---|---|---|---|---|
| Advance_Planning | Male | 100 | 3.64 | 1.194 | .119 |
|  | Female | 100 | 3.61 | 1.171 | .117 |
| Confidence | Male | 100 | 3.65 | 1.086 | .109 |
|  | Female | 100 | 3.52 | 1.114 | .111 |
| Persistent | Male | 100 | 3.74 | 1.125 | .112 |
|  | Female | 100 | 3.69 | 1.152 | .115 |

## Table No. 4.9: Group Statistics for Conviction between male & female leaders as perceived by leaders

The mean value shown above clearly shows that the males and females have similar opinions in different attribute of Conviction between male & female leaders as perceived by leaders like "I plan in advance for the possible outcomes through clarity in thoughts and actions", "I am confident about the situation whatever it may be", "I am persistent in achieving the targets", etc.

| | | Levene's Test for Equality of Variances | | t-test for Equality of Means | | | | | | | |
|---|---|---|---|---|---|---|---|---|---|---|---|
| | | F | Sig. | t | Df | Sig. (2-tailed) | Mean Differ ence | Std. Error Differ ence | 95% Confidence Interval of Difference | |
| | | | | | | | | | Lower | Upper |
| Developing_ Cooperation | Equal variances assumed | .238 | .626 | .874 | 198 | .383 | .130 | .149 | -.163 | .423 |
| | Equal variances not assumed | | | .874 | 197.832 | .383 | .130 | .149 | -.163 | .423 |
| Commitment | Equal variances assumed | .005 | .945 | .060 | 198 | .952 | .010 | .167 | -.319 | .339 |
| | Equal variances not assumed | | | .060 | 197.994 | .952 | .010 | .167 | -.319 | .339 |
| Team Based RewardSystem | Equal variances assumed | 2.668 | .104 | 1.579 | 198 | .116 | .250 | .158 | -.062 | .562 |
| | Equal variances not assumed | | | 1.579 | 195.969 | .116 | .250 | .158 | -.062 | .562 |
| Caring Approach | Equal variances assumed | .000 | .993 | 1.073 | 198 | .285 | .180 | .168 | -.151 | .511 |
| | Equal variances not assumed | | | 1.073 | 197.834 | .285 | .180 | .168 | -.151 | .511 |
| Belongingness | Equal variances assumed | .000 | .996 | 1.067 | 198 | .287 | .180 | .169 | -.153 | .513 |
| | Equal variances not assumed | | | 1.067 | 197.816 | .287 | .180 | .169 | -.153 | .513 |

**Table No. 4.14: Independent Samples Test for Team Work Spirit between male & female leaders as perceived by leaders**

The above table shows the levene's test of equality of variance & t test. The P value of levene's test is higher than 0.05 for $1^{st}$ & $3^{rd}$ attribute of Team Work Spirit, so equal variance are assumed for these cases. The respective p values for t test are 0.383 and 0.116. The P value of levene's test is less than 0.05 for $2^{nd}$, $4^{th}$ and $5^{th}$ attribute of Team Work Spirit, so equal variance are not assumed for this case, the respective t test p value for the same are 0.952, 0.285 and 0.287. So, test is accepted for all the variables so we can say that the hypothesis is accepted. Hence there is no significant difference in Team working spirit between male and female leaders as perceived by leaders.

**H$_{6.2}$: There is no significant difference in Team working spirit between male and female leaders as perceived by subordinates.**

|  | Gender | N | Mean | Std. Deviation | Std. Error Mean |
|---|---|---|---|---|---|
| Developing Cooperation | Male | 100 | 3.58 | 1.037 | .104 |
|  | Female | 100 | 3.35 | 1.123 | .112 |
| Commitment | Male | 100 | 3.66 | 1.233 | .123 |
|  | Female | 100 | 3.66 | 1.216 | .122 |
| Team Based Reward System | Male | 100 | 3.71 | 1.131 | .113 |
|  | Female | 100 | 3.46 | 1.234 | .123 |
| Caring Approach | Male | 100 | 3.29 | 1.192 | .119 |
|  | Female | 100 | 3.10 | 1.243 | .124 |
| Belongingness | Male | 100 | 3.36 | 1.202 | .120 |
|  | Female | 100 | 3.20 | 1.198 | .120 |

## Table No. 4.15: Group Statistics for Team Work Spirit between male & female leaders as perceived by Subordinates

The table talks about the variables like mean, standard deviation, std. error, etc. In case of the attribute "Team Work Spirit" between male & female leaders as perceived by their subordinates, the mean value of male & female are in between 3 and 4 which gives two indications, firstly they have same opinion and secondly subordinates have shown their agreement for Team Work Spirit of their leaders. The values of standard deviation are also very less which means low degree of variability in their responses.

| | | Levene's Test for Equality of Variances | | t-test for Equality of Means | | | | | 95% Confidence Interval of the Difference | |
|---|---|---|---|---|---|---|---|---|---|---|
| | | F | Sig. | T | df | Sig. (2-tailed) | Mean Differ ence | Std. Error Differ ence | Lower | Upper |
| Developing Cooperation | Equal variances assumed | .750 | .388 | 1.505 | 198 | .134 | .230 | .153 | -.071 | .531 |
| | Equal variances not assumed | | | 1.505 | 196.754 | .134 | .230 | .153 | -.071 | .531 |
| Commitment | Equal variances assumed | .018 | .894 | .000 | 198 | 1.000 | .000 | .173 | -.341 | .341 |
| | Equal variances not assumed | | | .000 | 197.964 | 1.000 | .000 | .173 | -.341 | .341 |
| Team Based Reward System | Equal variances assumed | 1.530 | .218 | 1.493 | 198 | .137 | .250 | .167 | -.080 | .580 |
| | Equal variances not assumed | | | 1.493 | 196.499 | .137 | .250 | .167 | -.080 | .580 |
| Caring Approach | Equal variances assumed | .003 | .959 | 1.103 | 198 | .271 | .190 | .172 | -.150 | .530 |
| | Equal variances not assumed | | | 1.103 | 197.647 | .271 | .190 | .172 | -.150 | .530 |
| Belongingness | Equal variances assumed | .119 | .730 | .943 | 198 | .347 | .160 | .170 | -.175 | .495 |
| | Equal variances not assumed | | | .943 | 197.997 | .347 | .160 | .170 | -.175 | .495 |

## Table No. 4.16: Independent Samples Test for Team Work Spirit between male & female leaders as perceived by Subordinates

The p value in levene's test of equality is higher than 0.05 except in 4th attribute of Team Work Spirit. So for attribute "the leader is considerate and has a caring approach towards us in solving problems", we will look at equal variances not assumed i.e. bottom row for t test result i.e. 0.271. For all the other attributes of Script equal variances are assumed & therefore upper row of t test will give the correct result. All the p value> 0.05 this indicates that there is no significant difference in Team working spirit between male and female leaders as perceived by subordinates. Hence the hypothesis is accepted.

**$H_{7.1}$: There is no significant difference in Decision making skills between male and female leaders as perceived by leaders.**

|  | Gender | N | Mean | Std. Deviation | Std. Error Mean |
|---|---|---|---|---|---|
| Clear Instruction Decision | Male | 100 | 3.98 | .985 | .098 |
|  | Female | 100 | 3.66 | 1.224 | .122 |
| Proper Commu Decision | Male | 100 | 3.37 | 1.031 | .103 |
|  | Female | 100 | 3.24 | 1.055 | .106 |
| Too Much Time_ Decision | Male | 100 | 3.50 | 1.059 | .106 |
|  | Female | 100 | 3.44 | 1.048 | .105 |
| Develop Structure Decision | Male | 100 | 3.59 | 1.093 | .109 |
|  | Female | 100 | 3.48 | 1.096 | .110 |
| AlignPersonalOrgGoals | Male | 100 | 3.62 | 1.153 | .115 |
|  | Female | 100 | 3.36 | 1.235 | .124 |

**Table No. 4.17: Group Statistics for Decision Making Skills between male & female leaders as perceived by leaders**

The mean for each of the two groups in the "Groups Statistics Section" shows that both males & females have approximately similar opinion in case of Decision Making Skills. The mean values of all attribute is close to 4 which means leaders have shown their agreement towards the attribute like "I instruct clearly to my subordinates for taking an immediate action", "I communicate properly regarding the implementation of decision", "I generally take too much time before making the decisions", "I develop structures to foster participation in decisions" etc. The standard deviation in all the cases is near to 1 which indicates less deviation in leader's opinion.

| | | Levene's Test for Equality of Variances | | t-test for Equality of Means | | | | | | | |
|---|---|---|---|---|---|---|---|---|---|---|---|
| | | F | Sig. | T | Df | Sig. (2-tailed) | Mean Difference | Std. Error Difference | 95% Confidence Interval of the Difference | | |
| | | | | | | | | | Lower | Upper | |
| Clear Instruction_ Decision | Equal variances assumed | 8.619 | .004 | 2.037 | 198 | .043 | .320 | .157 | .010 | .630 | |
| | Equal variances not assumed | | | 2.037 | 189.273 | .043 | .320 | .157 | .010 | .630 | |
| Proper Commu_ Decision | Equal variances assumed | .000 | .988 | .881 | 198 | .379 | .130 | .148 | -.161 | .421 | |
| | Equal variances not assumed | | | .881 | 197.896 | .379 | .130 | .148 | -.161 | .421 | |
| Too Much Time Decision | Equal variances assumed | .016 | .900 | .403 | 198 | .688 | .060 | .149 | -.234 | .354 | |
| | Equal variances not assumed | | | .403 | 197.977 | .688 | .060 | .149 | -.234 | .354 | |
| Develop Structure _Decision | Equal variances assumed | .000 | .984 | .711 | 198 | .478 | .110 | .155 | -.195 | .415 | |
| | Equal variances not assumed | | | .711 | 197.998 | .478 | .110 | .155 | -.195 | .415 | |
| Align Personal Org Goals | Equal variances assumed | .453 | .502 | 1.539 | 198 | .125 | .260 | .169 | -.073 | .593 | |
| | Equal variances not assumed | | | 1.539 | 197.064 | .125 | .260 | .169 | -.073 | .593 | |

**Table No. 4.18: Independent Samples Test for Decision Making Skills between male & female leaders as perceived by leaders**

The above table shows the levene's test of equality of variance & t test. The P value of levene's test is higher than 0.05 for 1st & 5th attribute of Decision Making Skills, so equal variance are assumed for these cases. The respective p values for t test are 0.043 and 0.125. The P value of levene's test is less than 0.05 for 2nd, 3rd & 4th attribute of Decision Making Skills, so equal variance are not assumed for this case, the respective t test p value for the same is 0.379, 0.688 and 0.125. So, test is accepted for majority of the variables so overall we can say that the hypothesis is accepted. Hence, there is no significant difference in Decision making skills between male and female leaders as perceived by leaders.

**H$_{7.2}$: There is no significant difference in Decision making skills between male and female leaders as perceived by subordinates**

|  | Gender | N | Mean | Std. Deviation | Std. Error Mean |
|---|---|---|---|---|---|
| Clear Instruction | Male | 100 | 3.94 | 1.023 | .102 |
| Decision | Female | 100 | 3.66 | 1.224 | .122 |
| Proper Commu | Male | 100 | 3.38 | 1.033 | .103 |
| Decision | Female | 100 | 3.20 | 1.082 | .108 |
| Too Much Time | Male | 100 | 3.36 | 1.115 | .111 |
| Decision | Female | 100 | 3.37 | 1.125 | .113 |
| Develop Structure | Male | 100 | 3.50 | 1.106 | .111 |
| Decision | Female | 100 | 3.39 | 1.171 | .117 |
| Align Personal Org | Male | 100 | 3.60 | 1.181 | .118 |
| Goals | Female | 100 | 3.11 | 1.392 | .139 |

## Table No. 4.19: Group Statistics for Decision Making Skills between male & female leaders as perceived by Subordinates

The above table provides very useful descriptive statistics, including the mean, standard deviation and Standard error. The mean scores are close to 4 which indicate that leaders irrespective of their gender similar opinion for transformational leadership attribute "Decision Making Skills" as perceived by their subordinates. The column standard deviation depicts the variability in the data which is of low degree.

| | | Levene's Test for Equality of Variances | | t-test for Equality of Means | | | | | | 95% Confidence Interval of the Difference | |
|---|---|---|---|---|---|---|---|---|---|---|---|
| | | F | Sig. | T | df | Sig. (2-tailed) | Mean Difference | Std. Error Difference | | Lower | Upper |
| Clear Instruction _Decision | Equal variances assumed | 5.558 | .019 | 1.755 | 198 | .081 | .280 | .160 | | -.035 | .595 |
| | Equal variances not assumed | | | 1.755 | 191.938 | .081 | .280 | .160 | | -.035 | .595 |
| Proper Commu _Decision | Equal variances assumed | .027 | .869 | 1.203 | 198 | .230 | .180 | .150 | | -.115 | .475 |
| | Equal variances not assumed | | | 1.203 | 197.561 | .230 | .180 | .150 | | -.115 | .475 |
| Too Much Time Decision | Equal variances assumed | .014 | .907 | -.063 | 198 | .950 | -.010 | .158 | | -.322 | .302 |
| | Equal variances not assumed | | | -.063 | 197.983 | .950 | -.010 | .158 | | -.322 | .302 |
| Develop Structure_ Decision | Equal variances assumed | .217 | .642 | .683 | 198 | .495 | .110 | .161 | | -.208 | .428 |
| | Equal variances not assumed | | | .683 | 197.345 | .495 | .110 | .161 | | -.208 | .428 |
| AlignPersonal OrgGoals | Equal variances assumed | 2.723 | .100 | 2.685 | 198 | .008 | .490 | .183 | | .130 | .850 |
| | Equal variances not assumed | | | 2.685 | 192.869 | .008 | .490 | .183 | | .130 | .850 |

**Table No. 4.20: Independent Samples Test for Decision Making Skills between male & female leaders as perceived by leaders**

The p value in levene's test of equality is higher than 0.05 except in 1ˢᵗ attribute of Decision Making Skills. So for attribute "He/she instructs clearly to the subordinates for taking an immediate action", we will look at equal variances not assumed i.e. bottom row for t test result i.e. 0.081. For all the other attributes of Script equal variances are assumed & therefore upper row of t test will give the correct result. So, test is accepted for majority of the variables, so overall we can say that the hypothesis is accepted. Hence, there is no significant difference in Decision making skills between male and female leaders as perceived by subordinates.

**H₈.₁:** **There is no significant difference in Attitude towards risk taking between male and female leaders as perceived by leaders**

|  | Gender | N | Mean | Std. Deviation | Std. Error Mean |
|---|---|---|---|---|---|
| Remove Risk | Male | 100 | 3.58 | 1.199 | .120 |
|  | Female | 100 | 3.11 | 1.392 | .139 |
| Calculated Risk | Male | 100 | 3.56 | 1.192 | .119 |
|  | Female | 100 | 3.13 | 1.368 | .137 |
| Reasonable Risk | Male | 100 | 3.60 | 1.172 | .117 |
|  | Female | 100 | 3.10 | 1.367 | .137 |
| High Risk for High Return | Male | 100 | 3.60 | 1.181 | .118 |
|  | Female | 100 | 3.11 | 1.385 | .138 |

**Table No. 4.21: Group Statistics for Attitude towards Risk between male & female leaders as perceived by leaders**

The descriptive output gives the sample size, mean, standard deviation and standard error. In the above table, all the mean score are in between 3 to 4 which means leaders have shown their agreement in terms of Attitude towards Risk but if we observe the values mean score of males are near to 4 and mean scores of female is near to 3 which shows varying opinion of leaders in terms of attitude towards risk.

The p value of Levene' s test in all the attributes of Attitude towards Risk is not less than .05, so the equal variances are assumed. The p values of the t test of the upper rows are less than .05 in all the cases, which means that there is a significant difference in Attitude towards risk taking between male and female leaders as perceived by leaders. Hence the hypothesis is rejected.

**$H_{8.2}$: There is no significant difference in Attitude towards risk taking between male and female leaders as perceived by subordinates**

The mean & standard deviation of transformational leadership attribute known as "Attitude towards Risk" of male & female leaders as perceived by their subordinates. The mean value of male is on higher side of agreement while the mean value of female is on lower side of agreement which depicts that the subordinates have different opinion in terms of risk taking attitude of their leaders.

The p value of Levene's test in all the attributes of Attitude towards Risk is not less than .05, so the equal variances are assumed. The p values of the t test of the upper rows are less than .05 in all the cases, which means that there is a significant difference in Attitude towards risk taking between male and female leaders as perceived by subordinates. Hence the hypothesis is rejected.

**$H_{9.1}$: There is no significant difference in Conflict management approach between male and female leaders as perceived by leaders**

The output of independent samples of t test in SPSS gives the result of Levene's test for the equality of variances & t test for equality of means. The p value in levene's test of equality is higher than 0.05 except in $2^{nd}$ attribute of Conflict Management. So for attribute "I encourage constructive conflicts, provided it leads to new ideas", we will look at equal variances not assumed i.e. bottom row for t test result i.e. 0.739. For all the other attributes of Script equal variances are assumed & therefore upper row of t test will give the correct result. So, test is accepted for majority of the variables, so overall we can say that the hypothesis is accepted. Hence, there is no significant difference in

Conflict Management between male and female leaders as perceived by leaders.

**H$_{9.2}$: There is no significant difference in Conflict management approach between male and female leaders as perceived by subordinates**

The mean values of different attributes of Conflict Management between male & female leaders as perceived by their subordinates. The mean value in case of "I am always prepared to listen to alternative suggestions" is close to 3 which indicates their neutral opinion while in other attributes like "I am able to manage conflicts very well most of the time, I encourage constructive conflicts, provided it leads to new ideas, I feel reasonably relaxed about conflict, provided I have the situation under my control" the mean value is close to 4 which shows agreement of leaders for the above factors irrespective of their gender.

The independent sample t test shows two tests i.e. Levene's test & T test. Levene's test is for equality of variances. If the significance value is less than .05, variances are not assumed to be equal. One of the attribute i.e. "He/ she is always prepared to listen to alternative suggestions" from Conflict Management have significance value less than .05. Hence the variances of these values assumed not to be equal. But significance values of t test of all variables irrespective of their variances, are higher than .05 which means there is no significant difference in Conflict management approach between male and female leaders as perceived by subordinates. So the hypothesis stands accepted.

**H$_{10.1}$: There is no significant difference in People development style between male and female leaders as perceived by leaders**

The group statistics of one of the attribute of transformational leadership called People Development Style on the basis of gender as perceived by leaders. The mean value of male and female seems to be same which shows their similar opinion for People Development Style. The values of standard deviation are also very less which shows low degree of variation in their responses.

The p value of Levene's test in all the attributes of People Development Style is not less than .05, so the equal variances are assumed. The p values of the t test of the upper rows are higher than .05 in all the cases, which means that there is no significant difference in People development style between male and female leaders as perceived by leaders. Hence the hypothesis is accepted.

**$H_{10.2}$: There is no significant difference in People development style between male and female leaders as perceived by subordinates**

The Group Statistics table shows the mean & standard deviation of different attribute of People Development Style on the basis of gender as perceived by their subordinates. We can observe from the above table that the mean value of males & females are almost same which indicates male & female leaders are same in terms of transformational People Development Style.

The output of independent samples of t test in SPSS gives the result of Levene's test for the equality of variances & t test for equality of means. The p value in levene's test of equality is higher than 0.05 except in 4th attribute of People Development Style. So for attribute "He/she believes in result oriented approach", we will look at equal variances not assumed i.e. bottom row for t test result i.e. 0.069. For all the other attributes of People Development Style equal variances are assumed & therefore upper row of t test will give the correct result. So, test is accepted for majority of the variables, so overall we can say that the hypothesis is accepted. Hence, there is no significant difference in People development style between male and female leaders as perceived by subordinates.

**H$_{11.1}$: There is no significant difference in Autonomy between male and female leaders as perceived by leaders**

It is clear that the males and females have approximately similar opinions in different attribute of Autonomy between male & female leaders as perceived by leaders like "I improve the performance and commitment level through good supervision", "Self-starters are always encouraged by me", except "I provide adequate authority and set the objectives for planning & implementation of strategies" where we can notice slightly different opinion.

The Levene's test of equality & t test. The p value of Levene' s test in all the attributes of Autonomy is not less than .05, so the equal variances are assumed. The p values of the t test of the upper rows are not less than .05 in all the cases, which means that there is no significant difference in Autonomy between male and female leaders as perceived by leaders. Hence the hypothesis stands accepted.

**H$_{11.2}$: There is no significant difference in Autonomy between male and female leaders as perceived by subordinates**

This talks about the descriptive statistics on the basis of group called Gender. The males and females have approximately the same opinion in all the attributes of direction except "Leader provides adequate authority and objectives for planning & implementation of strategies". The values of standard deviation are also very less which indicates that low degree of variation in the responses of leaders as perceived by their subordinates.

The result of independent samples of t test in SPSS gives the result of Levene's test for the equality of variances & t test for equality of means. The p value of Levene's test is higher than .05 except for the 1st attribute "Leader provides adequate authority and objectives for planning & implementation of strategies" so in this case equal variance is not assumed. For rest of the attributes where p value of levene's test is higher than 0.05, equal variances are assumed. Now if look at the respective p value of t test, we can observe that "there is a significant difference in adequate authority between male and female leaders as perceived by subordinates" and for rest of the variables "there is no significant difference in attribute like good supervision and self starters between male and female leaders as perceived by subordinates". So, test is accepted for majority of the variables so overall we can say that the hypothesis is accepted.

**$H_{12.1}$: There is no significant difference in Nurturing style between male and female leaders as perceived by leaders.**

The male & female leaders have same opinion in attribute of Nurturing Style like "My leader always extends helping hands to team members", "My leader tries to help in improving the shortcomings of subordinates", "He/she always gives credit to those who perform better", "He/she is sensitive to our personal needs", "My leader has full faith in the ability of team members".

To see the result of Independent Sample t test, first we have to look for the "Levene's Test for Equality of Variance" section. The p values for variances are 0.001, 0.019, 0.039, 0.152 & 0.020 all are less than .05 except 4th value, therefore for 4th attribute "I am sensitive to personal needs of team members." we have assumed equal variance & we will look at the top row for t test result. And for all other cases equal variances are not assumed. The p values irrespective of their respective variances are not less than 0.05 which indicates that there is no significant difference in Nurturing style between male and female leaders as perceived by leaders. Hence the hypothesis stands accepted.

**$H_{12.2}$: There is no significant difference in Nurturing style between male and female leaders as perceived by subordinates.**

The males and females have approximately the same opinion in all the attributes of direction. The values of standard deviation are also very less which indicates that low degree of variation in the responses of leaders as perceived by their subordinates.

To read the result of Independent Sample t test, first we have to look for the "Levene's Test for Equality of Variance" section. All p values for variances are less than .05 except $2^{nd}$ variable, therefore for $2^{nd}$ variable "My leader tries to help in improving the shortcomings of subordinates" we have assumed equal variance & we will look at the top row for t test result. And for all other cases equal variances are not assumed. The p values irrespective of their respective variances are not less than 0.05 which indicates that there is no significant difference in Nurturing style between male and female leaders as perceived by subordinates. Hence the hypothesis stands accepted.

**$H_{12.2}$: There is no significant difference in Nurturing style between male and female leaders as perceived by subordinates**

The males and females have approximately the same opinion in all the attributes of direction. The values of standard deviation are also very less which indicates that low degree of variation in the responses of leaders as perceived by their subordinates.

To read the result of Independent Sample t test, first we have to look for the "Levene's Test for Equality of Variance" section. All p values for variances are less than .05 except $2^{nd}$ variable, therefore for $2^{nd}$ variable "My leader tries to help in improving the shortcomings of subordinates" we have assumed equal variance & we will look at the top row for t test result. And for all other cases equal variances are not assumed. The p values irrespective of their respective variances are not less than 0.05 which indicates that there is no significant difference in Nurturing style between male and female leaders as perceived by subordinates. Hence the hypothesis stands accepted.

**$H_{13.1}$: There is no significant difference in Organizational commitment between male and female leaders as perceived by leaders**

The mean for each of the two groups in the "Groups Statistics Section" shows that both males & females have approximately similar opinion in case of Organizational Commitment. The mean values of all attribute is between 3 to 4 which means leaders have shown their agreement towards the attribute like "I believe that relationship is developed through the involvement of employees in decision making", "Organization policies play an important role in increasing the commitment level of employees", "I am always prepared to listen to alternative suggestions", "I develop structures to foster participation in decisions", "On duty, I give priority to my organizational work rather than personal work". The standard deviation in all the cases is near to 1 which indicates less deviation in leader's opinion.

The result of independent samples of t test in SPSS gives the result of Levene's test for the equality of variances & t test for equality of means. The p value of Levene's test is higher than .05 except for the two attribute namely "I am always prepared to listen to alternative suggestions "and "I try to promote quality of work life in the organization" so in these cases equal variances are not assumed. For rest of the attributes where p value of levene's test is higher than 0.05, equal variances are assumed. Now if look at the respective p value of t test, we can observe that all p value are higher than 0.05 and we can conclude that there is no significant difference in Organizational commitment between male and female leaders as perceived by leaders. So, we can say that the hypothesis is accepted.

**$H_{13.2}$: There is no significant difference in Organizational commitment between male and female leaders as perceived by subordinates**

The mean scores are close to 4 which indicate that leaders irrespective of their gender similar opinion for transformational leadership attribute "Organizational Commitment" as perceived by their subordinates. The column standard deviation depicts the variability in the data which is of low degree.

The result shows the Levene's test of equality & t test. The p value of Levene' s test in all the attributes of Attitude towards Risk is not less than .05, so the equal variances are assumed. The p values of the t test of the upper rows are not less than .05 in all the cases, which means that there is no significant difference in Organizational commitment between male and female leaders as perceived by subordinates. Hence the hypothesis stands accepted.

**$H_{14.1}$: There is no significant difference in extent of Optimism between male and female leaders as perceived by leaders**

The mean & standard deviation of different attribute of Optimism on the basis of gender as perceived by them.

We can observe from the above table that the mean value of males & females are almost same which indicates male & female leaders are same in terms of transformational Optimism Approach.

The p value of Levene' s test in all the attributes of Attitude towards Risk is not less than .05, so the equal variances are assumed. The p values of the t test of the upper rows are not less than .05 in all the cases, which means that there is no significant difference in extent of Optimism between male and female leaders as perceived by leaders. Hence the hypothesis stands accepted.

$H_{14.2}$: **There is no significant difference in extent of Optimism between male and female leaders as perceived by subordinates**

The mean & standard deviation of transformational Optimism Approach of male & female leaders as perceived by their subordinates. The mean value of male is approximately same as the mean value of female which depicts that the subordinates have similar opinion in terms of optimism approach of leaders as perceived by their subordinates.

The result of independent samples t test in SPSS in the form of Levene's test for the equality of variances & t test for equality of means. The p value of Levene's test is higher than .05, so equal variances are assumed. Now if look at the respective p value of t test, we can observe that all p value are higher than 0.05 and we can conclude that There is no significant difference in extent of Optimism between male and female leaders as perceived by subordinates. So, we can say that the hypothesis is accepted.

$H_{15.1}$: **There is no significant difference in Performance-oriented approach between male and female leaders as perceived by leaders**

The p value of Levene' s test in all the attributes of Performance Oriented Approach is not less than .05, so the equal variances are assumed. The p values of the t test of the upper rows are not less than .05 in all the cases, which means that there is no significant difference in Performance-oriented approach between male and female leaders as perceived by leaders. Hence the hypothesis stands accepted.

**$H_{15.2}$: There is no significant difference in Performance-oriented approach between male and female leaders as perceived by subordinates**

The result of independent samples of t test in SPSS gives the result of Levene's test for the equality of variances & t test for equality of means. The p value of Levene's test is less than .05 except for one attribute i.e." He/she asks for regular updates & makes sure that things are on track." so in this case equal variance is assumed. For rest of the attributes where p value of levene's test is less than 0.05, equal variances are not assumed. Now if look at the respective p value of t test, we can observe that all p value are higher than 0.05 and we can conclude that there is no significant difference in Performance-oriented approach between male and female leaders as perceived by subordinates So, we can say that the hypothesis is accepted.

**$H_{16.1}$: There is no significant difference in Assertiveness style between male and female leaders as perceived by leaders**

The descriptive output gives the sample size, mean, standard deviation and standard error. In the above table, all the mean score are in between 3 to 4 which means leaders have shown their agreement in terms of "Assertiveness Style" but if we observe, the mean score of males are near to 4 and mean scores of female are near to 3.5 which shows varying opinion of leaders in terms of Assertiveness Style.

The p value of Levene' s test in all the attributes of Assertiveness Style is not less than .05, so the equal variances are assumed. The p values of the t test of the upper rows are also less than .05 in all the cases, which means that there is a significant difference in Assertiveness Style between male and female leaders as perceived by leaders. Hence the hypothesis is rejected.

**$H_{16.2}$: There is no significant difference in Assertiveness style between male and female leaders as perceived by subordinates**

This explains the mean & standard deviation of transformational leadership attribute known as "Assertiveness Style" of male & female leaders as perceived by their subordinates. The mean value of male is on higher side of agreement while the mean value of female is on lower side of agreement which depicts that the subordinates have different opinion in terms of assertiveness style of their leaders.

The p value of Levene's test in all the attributes of Assertiveness Style is less than .05, so the equal variances are not assumed. The p values of the t test of the bottom rows are less than .05 in all the cases, which means that there is a significant difference in Assertiveness Style between male and female leaders as perceived by subordinates. Hence the hypothesis is rejected.

**$H_{17}$: There is no significant difference in transformational leadership approach between Private and Public Organizational leaders as perceived by them.**

From the analysis of hypothesis where we have analyzed significant difference between different transformational leadership approach between Private & Public

Organizational leaders as perceived by them, we can observe that out of 14 hypothesis, 7 stands accepted and 7 are rejected that indicates among various variables pertaining to transformational leadership 50 % carries similar opinion of leaders & another 50 % carries difference in opinion in terms of nature of organization, so we can conclude that on some variables there is a significant difference in transformational leadership approach between Private & Public organizational leaders as perceived by them, while on others there is no significant difference in transformational leadership approach between Private & Public organizational leaders as perceived by them. Hence within this hypothesis, 7 are accepted and 7 rejected.

**$H_{18}$: There is no significant difference in transformational leadership approach between Private and Public Organizational leaders as perceived by their subordinates**

From the analysis of hypothesis where we have analyzed significant difference between different transformational leadership approach between Private & Public Organizational leaders as perceived by subordinates, we can observe that out of 14 hypothesis, 8 stands accepted and 6 are rejected that indicates among various variables pertaining to transformational leadership few carries similar opinion of leaders & another few carries difference in opinion in terms of nature of organization, so we can conclude that on some variables there is a significant difference in transformational leadership approach between Private & Public organizational leaders as perceived by subordinates, while on others there is no significant difference in transformational leadership approach between Private & Public organizational leaders as perceived by subordinates. But because majority of the sub hypothesis are accepted, we can conclude that overall hypothesis stands accepted.

**$H_{19.1}$: There is no significant difference in Open communication approach between Private and Public Organizational leaders as perceived by leaders**

This talks about descriptive statistics which shows the values of mean & standard deviation. The transformational leaders have shown their agreement irrespective of their type of organization in all the attributes of Open Communication.

The result of Independent Sample t test, first we have to look for the "Levene's Test for Equality of Variance" section. The p values for variance are 0.913, 0.051, 0.000 & 0.167, first, second & fourth attribute have values higher than .05, therefore for t test we have assumed equal variance & we will look at the top row for t test result. The respective p values for t test are 0.435, 0.065 and 0.026 which indicates that out of three attributes two indicates that there is no significant difference in Open communication approach between Private & Public Organizational leaders as perceived by leaders. For third attribute "Open Door Policy" significance value of F test is 0.000, which means for t test we have to assume bottom row. The respective p value is 0.678 which again indicates no significant difference. Hence the hypothesis stands accepted.

**$H_{19.2}$: There is no significant difference in Open communication approach between Private and Public Organizational leaders as perceived by subordinates**

This shows the mean values of different attributes of Open Communication Approach between Private & Public Organizational leaders as perceived by their subordinates. The mean value in case of "My questions are being answered openly and honestly" is close to 3 which indicates their neutral opinion while in other attributes like "Policies and procedures are explained to me well by my leader/ supervisor, My leader encourages free and frank communication at various levels" the mean value is close to 4 which shows agreement of leaders for the above factors irrespective of their type of organization.

The Independent Sample t test shows two test i.e. Levene's test for equality of variances & t test. In Levene's test if the p value is less than .05, equal variance are not assumed. In all the cases the p value>0.05 except "My leader encourages free and frank communication at various levels", so for majority attributes variances are assumed equal. But irrespective of result of F test, all the values of t test are higher than .05 which means there is no significant difference in Open communication approach between Private & Public Organizational leaders as perceived by subordinates. Hence the hypothesis is accepted.

**$H_{20.1}$: There is no significant difference in Delegation style between Private and Public Organizational leaders as perceived by leaders**

This shows the levene's test of equality of variance & t test. The P value of levene's test is less than 0.05 in majority of the attributes of Delegation Style, so equal variances are not assumed for those cases. The respective p values for t test are 0.004, 0.050, 0.011, and 0.77. The P value of t test is again less than 0.05 in majority of the cases. So, test is rejected for three of the attributes. Hence, there is a significant difference in Delegation Style between Private and Public Organizational leaders as perceived by leaders.

**$H_{20.2}$: There is no significant difference in Delegation style between Private and Public Organizational leaders as perceived by subordinates**

The p value of Levene's test is higher than 0.05 for two cases and less than 0.05 for other two cases. Where p value is higher than 0.05, we will assume equal variance & for vice versa we will assume unequal variance. The majority of the p values of t test of are higher than .05, which means that there is no significant difference in Delegation Style between Private and Public Organizational leaders as perceived by subordinates. Hence the hypothesis is partially accepted.

**$H_{21.1}$: There is no significant difference in Conviction between Private and Public Organizational as perceived by leaders**

The p value in levene's test of equality is less than 0.05 in case of "I plan in advance for the possible outcomes through clarity in thoughts and actions and I am confident about the situation whatever it may be". So, we cannot assume equal variances assumed i.e. bottom row for t test result. The respective p values are 0.001 and 0.654. The p value of the third attribute is 0.238, this indicates that for majority of the attribute there is no significant difference in Conviction style between Private and Public Organizational leaders as perceived by leaders. Hence the hypothesis is accepted.

**$H_{21.2}$: There is no significant difference in Conviction between Private and Public Organizational leaders as perceived by subordinates**

The P value of levene's test is higher than 0.05 in most of the attributes of Conviction, so equal variances are assumed for those cases. The respective p values for t test are 0.007, 0.905, and 0.162. The P value of t test is higher than 0.05 except for first attribute. So, test is accepted for majority of the variables so overall we can say that the hypothesis is accepted. Hence, there is no significant difference in Conviction between Private and Public organizational leaders as perceived by subordinates.

**$H_{22.1}$: There is no significant difference in Team working spirit between Private and Public Organizational leaders as perceived by leaders**

The Private & Public Organizational leaders have same opinion in attribute of Team Work Spirit like "I am committed towards achieving the common goals", "Team based reward system is properly handled by me", "I am able to inculcate the sense of belongingness among the members of my team", but for few variables their view are varying like "I am capable enough to develop cooperation among the members", "I am considerate and have a caring approach towards my subordinates in solving the problems".

The output of independent samples of t test in SPSS gives the result of Levene's test for the equality of variances & t test for equality of means. The p value in levene's test of equality is higher than 0.05 in all the cases, so we will look at equal variances i.e. top row for t test result. The respective p values are 0.026, 0.952, 0.148, 0.017 and 0.408. Majority of the values are higher than 0.05, so the test is accepted for majority of the variables, so overall we can say that the hypothesis is accepted. Hence, there is no significant difference in Team Working Spirit between Private and Public Organizational leaders as perceived by leaders.

**$H_{22.2}$: There is no significant difference in Team working spirit between Private and Public Organizational leaders as perceived by subordinates**

The output of independent samples of t test in SPSS gives the result of Levene's test for the equality of variances & t test for equality of means. The p value in levene's test of equality is higher than 0.05 in all the cases, so we will look at equal variances i.e. top row for t test result. The respective p values are 0.005, 0.564, 0.171, 0.009 and 1.000. Majority of the values are higher than 0.05, so the test is accepted for majority of the variables, so overall we can say that the hypothesis is accepted. Hence, there is no significant difference in Team Working Spirit between Private and Public Organizational leaders as perceived by subordinates.

**$H_{23.1}$: There is no significant difference in Decision making skills between Private and Public Organizational leaders as perceived by leaders**

The P value of levene's test is higher than 0.05 for $3^{rd}$ , $4^{th}$ and $5^{th}$ attribute of Decision Making Skills, so equal variance are assumed for these cases. The respective p values for t test are 0.002, 0.003 and 0.000. The P value of levene's test is less than 0.05 for $1^{st}$ and $2^{nd}$ attribute of Decision Making Skills, so equal variance are not assumed for this case, the respective t test p value for the same are 1.000 and 0.000. So, test is rejected for majority of the variables so we can say that the hypothesis is rejected. Hence there is a significant difference in Decision Making Skill between Private and Public Organizational leaders as perceived by leaders.

**$H_{23.2}$: There is no significant difference in Decision making skills between Private and Public Organizational leaders as perceived by subordinates**

The P value of levene's test is higher than 0.05 for $3^{rd}$ and $4^{th}$ attribute of Decision Making Skills, so equal variance are assumed for these cases. The respective p values for t test are 0.001and 0.001. The P value of levene's test is less than 0.05 for $1^{st}$, $2^{nd}$ and $3^{rd}$ attribute of Decision Making Skills, so equal variance are not assumed for this case, the respective t test p value for the same are 1.000, 0.000 and 0.066. So, test is rejected for majority of the variables so we can say that the hypothesis is rejected. Hence there is a significant difference in Decision Making Skill between Private and Public Organizational leaders as perceived by subordinates.

**$H_{24.1}$: There is no significant difference in Attitude towards risk taking between Private and Public Organizational leaders as perceived by leaders**

The descriptive output gives the sample size, mean, standard deviation and standard error. In the above table, all the mean score are in between 3 to 4 which means leaders have shown their agreement in terms of Attitude towards Risk but if we observe the values mean score of private organizational are near to 4 and mean scores of public organizational leaders are near to 3 which shows varying opinion of leaders in terms of attitude towards risk.

The p value of Levene' s test in all the attributes of Attitude towards Risk is not less than .05, so the equal variances are assumed. The p values of the t test of the upper rows are less than .05 in all the cases, which means that there is a significant difference in Attitude towards risk taking between Private and Public Organizational leaders as perceived by leaders. Hence the hypothesis stands rejected.

**$H_{24.2}$: There is no significant difference in Attitude towards risk taking between Private and Public Organizational leaders as perceived by subordinates**

The p value of Levene's test in all the attributes of Attitude towards Risk is not less than .05, so the equal variances are assumed. The p values of the t test of the upper rows are less than .05 in all the cases, which means that there is a significant difference in Attitude towards risk taking between Private and Public Organizational leaders as perceived by subordinates. Hence the hypothesis is rejected.

**$H_{25.1}$: There is no significant difference in Conflict management approach between Private and Public Organizational leaders as perceived by leaders**

The output of independent samples of t test in SPSS gives the result of Levene's test for the equality of variances & t test for equality of means. The p value in levene's test of equality is higher than 0.05 in first two cases and it is lower than 0.05 for next two attributes of Conflict Management. So for attribute like "I am able to manage conflicts very well most of the time", "I encourage constructive conflicts, provided it leads to new ideas", we will look at equal variances assumed i.e. top row for t test result i.e. 0.065 and 0.386. For other attributes, unequal variances are assumed & therefore bottom row of t test will give the correct result. So, test is accepted for majority of the variables, so overall we can say that the hypothesis is accepted. Hence, there is no significant difference in Conflict Management between Private and Public Organizational leaders as perceived by leaders.

**$H_{25.2}$: There is no significant difference in Conflict management approach between Private and Public Organizational leaders as perceived by subordinates**

The mean value in case of "I am always prepared to listen to alternative suggestions" is close to 3 which indicates their neutral opinion while in other attributes like "I am able to manage conflicts very well most of the time, I encourage constructive conflicts, provided it leads to new ideas, I feel reasonably relaxed about conflict, provided I have the situation under my control" the mean value is close to 4 which shows agreement of leaders for the above factors irrespective of their nature of Organization.

The independent sample t test shows two tests i.e. Levene's test & T test. Levene's test is for equality of variances. If the significance value is less than .05, variances are not assumed to be equal. Two of the attribute i.e. "My leader feels reasonably relaxed about conflict, provided he/she has the situation under control" and "He/she is always prepared to listen to alternative suggestions" from Conflict Management have significance value less than .05. Hence the variances of these values assumed not to be equal. The respective significance values of t test are 0.012, 0.711, 0.003 and 0.130 which means there is partial significant difference in Conflict management approach between Private and Public Organizational leaders as perceived by subordinates. So the hypothesis stands partially accepted.

$H_{26.1}$: **There is no significant difference in People development style between Private and Public Organizational leaders as perceived by leaders**

The transformational leaders have shown their agreement irrespective of their type of organization in all the attributes of People Development Style except the case "I have empathy when others need help" where Private Organizational Leaders have mean near to neutral and Public Organizational Leaders have mean value near to agreement.

The p values for variance are 0.012, 0.015, 0.055 & 0.985, first and second attribute have values less than .05, therefore for t test we have assumed unequal variance & we will look at the bottom row for t test result. For other attribute we will look at the top row for t test result. The respective p values for t test are 0.096, 0.050, 0.005 and 0.521 which indicates that out of four attributes three indicates that there is no significant difference in People Development Style between Private & Public Organizational leaders as perceived by leaders. Hence the hypothesis stands accepted.

**H$_{26.2}$: There is no significant difference in People development style between Private and Public Organizational leaders as perceived by subordinates**

The transformational leaders have shown their agreement irrespective of their type of organization in all the attributes of People Development Style except the case "I have empathy when others need help" where Private Organizational Leaders have mean near to neutral and Public Organizational Leaders have mean value near to agreement as perceived by their subordinates.

The p values for variance are 0.078, 0.014, 0.115 & 0.355, the second attribute has value less than .05, therefore for t test we have assumed unequal variance & we will look at the bottom row for t test result. For other attribute we will look at the top row for t test result. The respective p values for t test are 0.094, 0.636, 0.018 and 0.950 which indicates that out of four attributes three indicates that there is no significant difference in People Development Style between Private & Public Organizational leaders as perceived by their subordinates. Hence the hypothesis stands accepted.

**H$_{27.1}$: There is no significant difference in Autonomy between Private and Public Organizational as perceived by leaders**

The mean value clearly shows that the Private and Public Organizational leaders have approximately similar opinions in different attribute of Autonomy as perceived by leaders like "I provide adequate authority and set the objectives for planning & implementation of strategies", "Self-starters are always encouraged by me", except "I improve the performance and commitment level through good supervision" where we can notice slightly different opinion.

The p value of Levene' s test in all the attributes of Autonomy is not less than .05 except the attribute "I provide adequate authority and set the objectives for planning & implementation of strategies" so where p value is less than 0.05, unequal variances are assumed and where it is higher than 0.05, equal variances are assumed. The respective p values of the t test are 0.598, 0.000 and 0.122 which means that for majority of the attributes there is no significant difference in Autonomy between Private and Public Organizational leaders as perceived by leaders. Hence the hypothesis stands accepted.

**$H_{27.2}$: There is no significant difference in Autonomy between Private and Public Organizational leaders as perceived by subordinates**

The Private and Public organizational leaders have approximately the same opinion in all the attributes of direction except "He/she improves the performance and commitment level through good supervision". The values of standard deviation are also very less which indicates that low degree of variation in the responses of leaders as perceived by their subordinates.

The result of independent samples of t test in SPSS gives the result of Levene's test for the equality of variances & t test for equality of means. The p value of Levene's test is less than .05 except for the 2nd attribute "He/she improves the performance and commitment level through good supervision" so in this case equal variance is assumed. For rest of the attributes where p value of levene's test is less than 0.05, equal variances are not assumed. Now if look at the respective p value of t test, we can observe that "there is a significant difference in good supervision between Private and Public organizational leaders as perceived by subordinates" and for rest of the variables "there is no significant difference in attribute like adequate authority and self starters between Private and Public organizational leaders as perceived by subordinates". So, test is accepted for majority of the variables so overall we can say that the hypothesis is accepted.

**$H_{28.1}$: There is no significant difference in Nurturing style between Private and Public Organizational as perceived by leaders**

The result of Independent Sample t test, first we have to look for the "Levene's Test for Equality of Variance" section. The p values for variance are 0.126, 0.965, 0.172, 0.945 and 0.005, all value are higher than .05 except the last one, therefore for t test we have assumed equal variance & we will look at the top row for t test result for all the values except last one. The respective p values for t test are 0.141, 0.000, 0.002, 0.171 and 0.019 which indicates that out of five attributes three indicates that there is a significant difference in Nurturing Style between Private & Public Organizational leaders as perceived by leaders. So for majority of the attribute, values are less than 0.05. Hence hypotheses stands rejected.

**$H_{28.2}$: There is no significant difference in Nurturing style between Private and Public Organizational as perceived by subordinates**

The result of Independent Sample t test, first we have to look for the "Levene's Test for Equality of Variance" section. The p values for variance are 0.092, 0.823, 0.172, 0.845 and 0.005, all value are higher than .05 except the last one, therefore for t test we have assumed equal variance & we will look at the top row for t test result for all the values except last one. The respective p values for t test are 0.281, 0.000, 0.002, 0.247 and 0.019 which indicates that out of five attributes three indicates that there is a significant difference in Nurturing Style between Private & Public Organizational leaders as perceived by subordinates. So for majority of the attribute, values are less than 0.05. Hence hypotheses stands rejected.

**$H_{29.1}$: There is no significant difference in Organizational commitment between Private and Public Organizational leaders as perceived by leaders**

The result of Independent Sample t test, first we have to look for the "Levene's Test for Equality of Variance" section. The p values for variance are 0.000, 0.533, 0.000, 0.000 and 0.000, all value are less than .05 except for one attribute, therefore for t test we have assumed unequal variance for majority of the variables & we will look at the bottom row for t test result for all the values except for the second attribute. The respective p values for t test are 0.000, 0.000, 0.003, 0.014 and 0.581 which indicates that out of five attributes three indicates that there is a significant difference in Organizational Commitment between Private & Public Organizational leaders as perceived by leaders. So for majority of the attribute, values are less than 0.05. Hence hypotheses stands rejected.

**$H_{29.2}$: There is no significant difference in Organizational commitment between Private and Public Organizational leaders as perceived by subordinates**

This explains the sample size, mean, standard deviation and standard error. Almost all the mean score are in between 3 to 4 which means leaders have shown their agreement in terms of organizational Commitment but if we observe the values, mean score of Private & Public Organizational Leaders are not approximating to each other for majority of the variable which shows varying opinion of leaders in terms of Organizational Commitment as perceived by their leaders.

The result of independent samples of t test in SPSS gives the result of Levene's test for the equality of variances & t test for equality of means. The p value of Levene's test is less than .05 except for the one attribute namely "Organization policies play an important role in increasing the commitment level of employees" so in that case equal variance is assumed. For rest of the attributes where p values of levene's test are less than 0.05, equal variances are not assumed. Now if look at the respective p value of t test, we can observe that all p value are less than 0.05 except for the one attribute and we can conclude that there is a significant difference in Organizational commitment between Private and Public Organizational leaders as perceived by subordinates. So, we can say that the hypothesis is rejected.

**$H_{30.1}$: There is no significant difference in extent of Optimism between Private and Public Organizational leaders as perceived by leaders**

The p value in levene's test of equality in two of the three cases is less than 0.05. So, we will look at unequal variances i.e. bottom row for those two cases and where p value is higher than 0.05, we will assume equal variance for t test result. All the respective p values of t test< 0.05 which indicates that there is a significant difference in Optimism Approach between Private and Public organizational leaders as perceived by leaders. Hence the hypothesis is rejected.

**$H_{30.2}$: There is no significant difference in extent of Optimism between Private and Public Organizational leaders as perceived by subordinates**

All the mean score are in between 2 to 3 which means leaders have shown either disagreement or their neutral opinion in terms of Optimism Approach and if we observe the values, mean scores of Private organizational leaders are near to 3 and mean scores of Public organizational leaders are near to 4 which shows varying opinion of leaders in terms Optimism Approach as perceived by subordinates.

The independent sample t test shows two tests i.e. Levene's test & T test. Levene's test is for equality of variances. If the significance value is less than .05, variances are not assumed to be equal and if higher than 0.05, variances are assumed to be equal. But significance values of t test of all variables irrespective of their variances are less than .05 which means there is a significant difference in Optimism Approach between Private and Public organizational leaders as perceived by subordinates. So the hypothesis stands rejected.

**H$_{31.1}$: There is no significant difference in Performance-oriented approach between Private and Public Organizational leaders as perceived by leaders**

The p value in levene's test of equality in two of the three cases is less than 0.05. So, we will look at unequal variances i.e. bottom row for those two cases and where p value is higher than 0.05, we will assume equal variance for t test result. All the p values of t test< 0.05 this indicates that there is a significant difference in Performance Oriented Approach between Private and Public organizational leaders as perceived by leaders. Hence the hypothesis is rejected.

**H$_{31.2}$: There is no significant difference in Performance-oriented approach between Private and Public Organizational leaders as perceived by subordinates**

The independent sample t test shows two tests i.e. Levene's test & T test. Levene's test is for equality of variances. If the significance value is less than .05, variances are not assumed to be equal and if higher than 0.05, variances are assumed to be equal. But significance values of t test of all variables irrespective of their variances are less than .05 which means there is a significant difference in Performance Oriented Approach between Private and Public organizational leaders as perceived by subordinates. So the hypothesis stands rejected.

**$H_{32.1}$: There is no significant difference in Assertiveness style between Private and Public Organizational leaders as perceived by leaders**

The mean value of Private and Public organizational leaders seems to be same which shows their similar opinion for Assertiveness Style. The values of standard deviation are also very less which shows low degree of variation in their responses.

The p value in levene's test of equality is higher than 0.05 in all the cases. So, we will look at equal variances assumed i.e. top row for t test result. All the p value of t test> 0.05 this indicates that there is no significant difference in Assertiveness style between Private and Public organizational leaders as perceived by leaders. Hence the hypothesis is accepted

**$H_{32.2}$: There is no significant difference in Assertiveness style between Private and Public Organizational leaders as perceived by subordinates**

For looking at the result of t test, first we have to assume for the variances with the help of levene's test for equality of variances. The p values of levene's test are higher than 0.05 in all the cases, so equal variances will be considered. So the respective t test p values are .168, .131, 0.072, 0.092, 0.133, 0.138, 0.154 and 0.105 which means there is no significant difference in Assertiveness style between Private and Public organizational leaders as perceived by subordinates. Hence the hypothesis stands accepted.

The current chapter concludes with detailed analysis of primary data, which paves the way for Discussion and Implications, which are included in further chapter.

# V

# DISCUSSION, IMPLICATIONS AND SUGGESTIONS

**5.1 DISCUSSION**:

The research focuses on transformational leadership style with respect to male and female leaders working in private and public sectors. There are three major aspects in this research: transformational leadership; Gender differences and public and private sector. The study covered opinions of leaders and their direct subordinates on common characteristics. These subordinates were reporting directly to their specific leader in an organization. In one organization, one leader was selected irrespective of the number of subordinates working under him/her. Under four broad characteristics, and further factors therein, the response was recorded. It was found that the response of leader and his/her subordinates was found same for the given statement. This shows the better understanding of the terms between the leader and the member.

With the help of 32 hypotheses, the leadership style effectiveness was determined. Here in the study, transformational leader was not an ordinary leader; he/she was able to prove his mettle in the organization. After deep study of the organization, the researcher has identified such transformational leaders and approached them for data collection. When most of the hypotheses were accepted, it shows that male and female leaders are same in terms of transformational leadership style. This study explainsIn terms of transformational leadership approach between male and female leaders in public and private organizations, there was no significant difference found. This was found same as per the response of the leaders themselves as well as their subordinates.

It shows that now the approach is same irrespective of the gender. Research in gender differences across communication styles has come to the conclusion that men tend to be self-assertive and view conversations as a means towards a tangible outcome, such as obtaining power or dominance (Maltz & Borker, 1982). Women, on the other hand, value cooperation, this communal orientation "involves a concern with others, selflessness, and a desire to be at one with others" (Mason, 1994). Females are also typically known to have a less clear focus on where the boundaries of their relationships end and their individual identities, defined in terms of relational bonds.

It shows that now the approach is same irrespective of the gender. Further, in terms of open communication, the leaders were having same approach whether it was male or female. In today's age, the communication matters to great extent and all the leaders had same approach. Open door policy has been encouraged by all such leaders.

When it comes to delegation style, both male and female leaders were found to have similar approach. Hence, no difference was found. There are many tasks which are handled through delegation and effective delegation ensures better results. This aspect has also covered control and supervision of the employees. Besides, conviction was also found same in male and female leaders. Similar study was conducted and the results of Eagly and Johannesen-Schmidt (2001) suggested that male managers, who scored higher in "management by exception" and laissez faire managerial style, tended to delegate more than their female equivalents. The level of passion and determination is now same in both genders in public and private sectors. Similarly, team working spirit was also exhibited same for both male and female leaders. Leaders were effectiveness in terms of cooperation among the team members.

In terms of decision making skills, there was no difference found among male and female. Likewise, conflict management was considered to be done effectively by both male and female leaders as perceived by them as well as their subordinates. Smooth management of the conflict in the interest of the organization is always promoted. In the book, Men are From Mars and Women are From Venus, John Gray (2004) wrote: Men mistakenly expect women to think, communicate, and react the way men do; women mistakenly expect men to feel, communicate, and respond the way women do. We have forgotten that men and women are supposed to be different. As a result our relationships are filled with unnecessary friction and conflict.

The overall trends showed that women were more concerned with both maintenance of interpersonal relationships and task accomplishment-a finding that both confirms and refutes the stereotypical view of women as leaders (conventional wisdom has it that women are more concerned with relationships than with task accomplishment). The strongest difference found was that women tended to adopt a more democratic or participative style, and men tended to adopt a more autocratic or directive style. Eagly and Johnson (1990) provide two possible explanations for this difference. First, women who have managed to succeed as leaders might have more highly developed interpersonal skills. The other explanation is that women are not accepted as readily as men as leaders and, as a result, have to allow input into their decision making. "Thus proceeding in a participative and collaborative mode may enable many female leaders to win acceptance from others, gain self-confidence, and thereby be effective. Because men are not so constrained by attitudinal bias, they are freer to lead in an autocratic and non-participative manner should they so desire.

Further, in terms of people development style, both type of leaders had same effectiveness in terms of empathy, result oriented approach and encouragement. When it came to autonomy, the leaders always believe in motivating the self-starters in the organization. This further supplements his/her nurturing style, where sensitivity to personal needs is given due importance by the leaders. Organizational commitment and extent of optimism were also considered in favour of the leaders as perceived by themselves and their subordinates while data collection. Lastly, performance-oriented approach was also found same, where the leaders follow the track of the work assigned. Turner (2008) suggested that future research should examine gender differences in commitment across different occupations and organizations.

However, when it comes to attitude towards risk taking and assertiveness style, significant differences were found among male and female leaders. These are the two areas, where male leaders scored higher than female leaders. Risk taking tendency was found more in male leaders as perceived by themselves and their subordinates. Degree of assertiveness was also found more in male leaders.

The previous study disclosed that Women are, overall, more expressive, tentative, and polite in conversation, while men are more assertive, and power-hungry (Basow & Rubenfield, 2003). Men and women also differ in their relations towards others in society: while women strive to be more social in their interactions with others, men value their independence (Miller, 1976) Degree of assertiveness was also found more in male leaders. In the same way the previous study focuses on the risk taking attitude and it is observed that women are usually found to be individually more risk-averse than men in experiments (Croson and Gneezy (2009), Eckel and Grossman (2008), it is natural to conjecture that women's risk-taking for others could be different than men's. As discussed in previous chapter, data analysis was done with comprehensive findings. This chapter discusses implications, suggestions and conclusions.

## 5.2 DETAILED DATA ANALYSIS RESULTS:

The comprehensive representation of the results and their interpretation is shown in the following section:

**$H_1$: There is no significant difference in transformational leadership approach between male and female leaders as perceived by them.**

From the below analysis of hypothesis where we have analyzed significant difference between different transformational leadership approach between male & female leaders as perceived by them, we can observe that out of 16 hypothesis, 14 stands accepted and 2 are rejected with respect to attitude towards risk & assertiveness style. As majority of the hypothesis are accepted, so we can conclude that there is no significant difference in transformational leadership approach between male and female leaders as perceived by them.

**$H_2$: There is no significant difference in transformational leadership approach between male and female leaders as perceived by their subordinates.**

From the below hypothesis testing, where we have analyzed significant difference between different transformational leadership approach between male & female leaders as perceived by subordinates, it was found that out of 16 hypotheses two hypotheses namely $H_{08}$ and $H_{16}$ were rejected and rest were accepted. It can be inferred that when it comes to transformational leadership, significant differences were found among male and female leaders with respect to attitude towards risk taking and assertiveness style. As majority of the hypothesis are accepted, so we can conclude that there is no significant difference in transformational leadership approach between male and female leaders as perceived by subordinates?

**$H_{13}$: There is no significant difference in transformational leadership approach between Private and Public Organizational leaders as perceived by them.**

From the below analysis of hypothesis where we have analyzed significant difference between different transformational leadership approach between Private & Public Organizational leaders as perceived by them, we can observe that out of 14 hypothesis, 7 stands accepted and

7 are rejected that indicates among various variables pertaining to transformational leadership 50 % carries similar opinion of leaders & another 50 % carries difference in opinion in terms of nature of organization, so we can conclude that on some variables there is a significant difference in transformational leadership approach between Private & Public organizational leaders as perceived by them, while on others there is no significant difference in transformational leadership approach between Private & Public organizational leaders as perceived by them. Hence within this hypothesis, 7 are accepted and 7 rejected.

**H$_{14}$: There is no significant difference in transformational leadership approach between Private and Public Organizational leaders as perceived by their subordinates**

From the below analysis of hypothesis where we have analyzed significant difference between different transformational leadership approach between Private & Public Organizational leaders as perceived by subordinates, we can observe that out of 14 hypothesis, 8 stands accepted and 6 are rejected that indicates among various variables pertaining to transformational leadership few carries similar opinion of leaders & another few carries difference in opinion in terms of nature of organization, so we can conclude that on some variables there is a significant difference in transformational leadership approach between Private & Public organizational leaders as perceived by subordinates, while on others there is no significant difference in transformational leadership approach between Private & Public organizational leaders as perceived by subordinates. But because majority of the sub hypothesis are accepted, we can conclude that overall hypothesis stands accepted.

To conclude it is said that our nation has given many strong Male and Female Leaders and in the recent we salute to our Honorable Prime Minister Mr. Narendra Modiji.

The authentic Independence came on 26 May 2014 when Narendra Modi sworn in as the Prime Minister of India, a decisive leader who has vowed to make India an economic super powerhouse. Modi's interaction with world leaders put India on a high pedestal as a bellwether in the world map to reckon with, and won the confidence of the foreign investors who considered investing in India will be remuneratively lucrative under the Modi regime. Narendra Modi knows how to execute, and has the mandate he needs to act so effectively.

Narendra Modi's single minded obsession and tireless work making India well developed country and make 1.25 billion people to partake in the benefits of the magnification is the trait of a good leader. There are certain characteristics found in some people that seem to naturally put them in a position where they're looked up to as a leader. There are some clear characteristics that are found in good leaders. These qualities can be developed or may be naturally part of their personality. Let us explore them further.

Chanakya said "In the happiness of his subjects lies his happiness; in their welfare his welfare; whatever pleases himself he shall not consider as good, but whatever pleases his subjects he shall consider as good". This statement has been proved by Honorable Prime Minister.

As far as women Leaders are concerned, India is leading one step ahead. Smt. Indira Gandhi, the greatest women leader had reshaped the fate of India. She was the nation's daughter, brought up under the close watch of both her father Jawaharlal Nehru, who was India's first Prime

Minister after decades of British rule, and her country. When Indira Gandhi (no relation to Mohandas Karamchand Gandhi) was elected Prime Minister in 1966, a TIME cover line read, "Troubled India in a Woman's Hands." Those steady hands went on to steer India, not without controversy, for much of the next two decades through recession, famine, the detonation of the nation's first atomic bomb, a corruption scandal and a civil war in neighboring Pakistan that, under her guidance, led to the creation of a new state, Bangladesh. By the time she was assassinated, in 1984, Gandhi was the world's longest-serving female Prime Minister, a distinction she holds to this day.

> *""A nation's strength ultimately consists in what it can do on its own, and not in what it can borrow from others." - Indira Gandhi"*

Even in the corporate world, there are many women have done a tremendous achievement and gain recognition worldwide. The managing director and CEO of India's second-largest bank explain how she balances the local and the global. **Chanda Kochhar, managing director and CEO of India's ICICI Bank, knows a thing or two** about leading in a volatile environment. A longtime ICICI executive, Kochhar helped guide the company successfully through a major strategic shift before being tapped to lead India's second-largest bank in 2009—during the height of the global financial crisis.

### 5.3: IMPLICATIONS OF THE STUDY

A research study has to present substantial implications significant for the leaders and their subordinates. Research work is complete if it offers suggestions and implications for the leaders and their subordinates associated directly or indirectly. These suggestions are based on the response of leaders and subordinates who work under the guidance of leaders. Such implications and suggestions, if properly implemented, will bring better results. This study offers suggestions and implications for leaders and their subordinates, which are presented in the following heads:

- The present study has concretized the Leadership role with a vision and mission which brought out qualitative improvement in their specific roles and responsibilities as and when ascribed.
- The present study is helpful to Leadership role across the country in any organization and even outside India for knowing the exact details of management from Indian perspective .
- Knowing the issues concerns getting to know different cultural groups, how they receive, process, and internalize information. The tenets of diversity can facilitate this process. Diversity goes beyond race, gender, and sexual orientation. It includes thinking patterns, speech patterns, and spatial orientations.
- Global leaders' effective use of information technology is important and relevant to global systems and to the relationships of cultural, political, and international understanding. When communication is mediated by technology, the cultural competencies required for cross-cultural communications change.

Working with others, leaders need to understand the difference between intention and impact. The impact of an action or behaviour is a function of that action. Thus, when one say he/she did not intend to say or do it. That does not mitigate the impact; nor does it take away the pain. The more leaders understand themselves, their motives, motivations, etc., the better equipped they will be in leading in a global world, especially a world where the political elements are at work.

## 5.4 SUGGESTIONS & RECOMMENDATIONS:

- Future Policing should be given topmost priority in changing present work culture. The police leaders must develop a wider vision and sense of direction to work out the strategy for meeting challenges ahead.Leaders should have training in management skills, technical, human and conceptual skills.
- The leaders can be encouraged to give attention to the views of the team members and make them available when they share their problems. Transformational leadership is more effective in getting extra effort, satisfaction, commitment, and effectiveness of subordinates than transactional leadership. The more the transformational leadership qualities, the more will be the subordinates' extra effort, commitment, satisfaction and effectiveness. Employees should realize that there is a whole world of opportunities for people who stick to one organization.
- Communications among employees in the company should be improved by promoting social media within the company, which would facilitate greater connectivity among them.
- Careers should be customized and investment should be made in the skill development of the employees.
- It is mainly the leadership behaviour of the managers/ team leaders that shapes the work culture of the company. Their role is that of leaders where they can

be instrumental in releasing the human potential of the organization. They should realize that their behaviour can make or mar the team which they lead or the unit which they head. So they should be democratic in behaviour and the organizational pattern should be centripetal and not centrifugal.

- Employees can be retained by providing adequate opportunities for career growth and opportunities, treat employees fairly – through compensation, rewards and recognition schemes, building an open environment and culture, providing competitive remuneration packages, clarifying job responsibilities, continuous training opportunities for skill upgradation.
- To sustain leadership commitment, provide executives with data that substantiates the value of talent management.
- **Subordinates must be provided a cooperative work environment so that they can sharpen their skills and competencies.**
- The transformational leaders must show their agreement for open communication approach in all the attributes. Leadership is contextual in nature. The leadership development fabric intertwines the social, economic, political and business climate strands to make the leadership style effective. Exclusive focus on the individual leader may result in the organization not being able to reach its desired level of progress. Training and development interventions would be more effective if they include both aspects of leadership development and leader development.
- The groups formed for Leadership development interventions need to include both males and females and not focus exclusively on either so that neither males

nor females are insulated from real world situations where they both will have to deal with the opposite gender.

- The leaders need to be self-aware regarding the communication needs of a leader. They need to recognize their strengths and weaknesses in everyday communication with a 360 degree view i.e. communication with Superiors, Subordinates and peers keeping in mind the organizational goals. The leaders need to keep in mind the five major interpersonal skills required, namely Teaming, Motivating, Listening, Providing Feedback, and Promoting and Managing Resistance to Change for enhancing the effectiveness of their transformational leadership style

- The study indicates that the Intervention Program has helped females too, to be effective transformational leaders thereby paving the way to organizations. Women leaders by harnessing their interpersonal communication skills can be effective transformational leaders.

- Interpersonal leadership communication is a process to be practised on an everyday basis for the potential transformational leader to be effective. This process will improve the Transformational leadership style in the Indian context of the potential leaders; engage the people working with them as a team, which is essential in today's' scenario where teaming has been rated as the most important skill for any leader.

It is established by this research that there is an improvement in the Transformational leadership style of females also. Hence, the potential female leaders need to cultivate their Transformational leadership style through the use of the five major interpersonal communication skills practiced in the intervention. Through the use of these major interpersonal communication skills females can make an impact as Transformational leaders in the Indian context. From the organizations' perspective: Leadership interventions must not be only for a select few. Organizations need to focus on leadership development at all levels for surviving, responding, stimulating growth and change. It would not be possible to fulfil these needs with only a few leaders at the helm of the organizations. b) Both male and female potential transformational leaders should be cultivated for the organizations to increase the depth and diversity of their pool of transformational leadership talent. c) The organizations can divide the Intervention into individual, separate modules for training purposes to overcome the lack of time and also to concentrate on those components and interpersonal skills which require more attention. d) The component of individualized consideration aspect will help organizations to harness the different capabilities of women as leaders and to make the most of the inputs of women as transformational leaders.

## 5.5 FUTURE SCOPE OF STUDY:

This study has been undertaken with respect to transformational leadership approaches among male and female leaders in private and public sector in Indore. Leaders working in six sectors were taken into consideration for primary data collection. For researchers, this study can be useful in many ways. Further research studies can be done on large sample size; more sectors can be considered and more cities can be included. Sector-wise comparison can also be done. This study covers gender as a major demographic variable. Detailed studies can be done with respect to other demographic variables like-qualification, experience etc.

## 5.6 LIMITATIONS OF THE STUDY:

The study also explores the dimensions of an effective transformational leadership style. Limitations of the study are as follows:

- The sample size finally selected for primary data collection was small, which may appear small to represent the population in the region.
- There may be a possibility of prejudice in the selection of respondents.
- There may be possibility of biasness from respondents in filling up of questionnaire.
- There may be the chances of extremity bias by the respondents.
- There may be time limitation with respondents.
- The findings of this study may not be generalized for other areas of the state and nation.

# REFERENCES & BIBLIOGRAPHY

# A


- Avolio, B.J., & Bass, B. M. (1999). Re-examining the components of transformational and transactional leadership using the multifactor leadership questionnaire. Journal of Occupational & Organizational Psychology, 72(4), 441-462.
- Bass, B.M. (1985). Leadership and performance beyond expectations. New York: Free Press. Bass.
- Bass M. (1988). From Transactional to Transformational Leadership. Learning to share the vision.
- B.M. (1990a). Bass and Stogdill's handbook of leadership: Theory, research and managerial applications (3$^{rd}$ ed.) New York: Free Press. Bass,
- B.M. (1990b). Editorial: Toward a meeting of minds. Leadership Quarterly, 1.
- Bass, B.M. (1997). Does the transactional–transformational paradigm transcend organizational and national boundaries? American Psychologist, 52(2), 130–139.
- Bass, B.M., Avolio, B.J., & Atwater, L. (1996). The transformational and transactional leadership of men and women. *International Review of Applied Psychology*, 45, 5–34.
- Bass, 1985;Kouzes and Posner, 1987 (Leadership and Performance Beyond Expectations, Free Press, NY, 1985, p. 17).
- Bass, B.M. and Avolio, B.J. (1990), "The implications of transactional and transformational leadership for individual, team, and organizational development", Research in Organizational Change and Development,

Vol. 4 No. 1, p. 231.

- Bermis and Nanus, Leaders , The strategies of taking charge, New York: Harper and Rowe 1985, p11985.
- Bennis, W.G. "Leadership Theory and Administrative Behaviour: The Problem of Authority," Administrative Science Quarterly, 4, 1959,
- B,J. Hodge and Johnson H,J., *Management of Organisational* Behaviour, John Wiley and Sons, New York, 1970, **p.** 250.
- Dubinsky, A., Yammarino, F., & Jolson, M. (1995). An examination of linkages between personal characteristics and dimensions of transformational leadership. *Journal of Business and Psychology*, 9, 315-335.
- Eagly, A. H., & Karau, S. J. (1991). Gender and emergence of leaders: Ameta analysis, *Journal of Personality and Social Psychology*, 60, 685-710.
- Eagly, A. H., & Johannesen-Schmidt, M. C. (2001). The leadership styles of women and men. *Journal of Social Issues, 57,* 781-797.
- Eagely, A. H., Johannesen-Schmidt, M. C. & Engen, M. L. V. (2003). transformational,
- Fiedler, F,E., A Theory of Leadership Effectiveness, McGraw Hill, New York, 1967.
- Gottlieb, T.W. (1990). Transactional and transformational leadership styles of chief and associate chief nurses in Department of Veterans' Affairs Medical Centers: A descriptive study. Doctoral dissertation, Columbia University, DC.
- Gregory, A. (1990). Three theoretical perspectives concerning women in management *Journal of Business Ethics,* 9, 257- 266.
- Hackman et al., 1992; Book, 2000
- Hartof, D., & Koopman, P. (1997).Transactional versus

transformational leadership: An leadership: An analysis of the MLQ. Journal of Occupational & Organizational Psychology, 70 (1), 19-34.

- Hersey, P. & Blanchard, K. H. (1977).Management of Organizational Behavior, 3$^{rd}$ Edition. Englewood Cliffs, N. J.: Prentice-Hall, Inc.Hall.
- Hollander, E.P., and Jullian J.W., "Contemporary Trends in the Analysis of Leadership rocesses," Psychological Bulletin, 71, 1996, pp.387-391.
- Ivancevich, Szilagyi and Wallace, *Organisation* Behaviour *and Performance,* p.273(Adopted from Dr. M.J. Mathew, "Organisation: Theory and Behaviour," RBSA Publishers, Jaipur, 1993, p,181)
- Jassawalla, A. R., & Sashittal, H. C. (2002). Cultures that support product innovation processes. *Academy of Management Executive,* 16, 42-54.
- Katz, D., & Kahn, R. L. (1978).The social psychology of organizations (2$^{nd}$ ed.). New York: Wiley.
- kakabadse and kakabadse, 1998 .Essence of leadership. London: International Thomson Business Press.
- kanungo and conger (1993).Promoting altruism as a corporate goal. Academy of Management Executive, 7(3), 37-48.
- Keith Davis, *Human Behaviour at work,* Tata McGraw-Hill Company Ltd., New Delhi, 1975, p,124
- Krantz, 3., & Gilmore, T. N. (1990). The splitting of leadership and management as a social defence. Human Relations, 43, 183-204.
- Koontz, H., & O'Donnell, C. 1955. Principles of management. New York: McGraw-Hill.
- Luthans, F. (2005).Organizational Behavior (10thed.). McGraw – Hill/ Irwin Publication. Mondy, R. W., & Premeaux, S. R. (1995). Management (7$^{th}$ ed.). Englewood-

Cliffs-New Jersey: Prentice-Hall.

- Lorber, J. (1994). *Paradoxes of gender*. New Haven: Yale University Press.
- London,Taylor, Philip A S. (1974) A new Dictionary of Economics. Routledge and Kegan Paul, London,The Bridge - Raising Issues for the Public Sector, Issue 5, July 2002.
- Ogbonna, E., & Harris, L. C. (2000). Leadership style, organizational culture and performance: Empirical evidence from UK companies. *International journal of Human Resource Management,*11(4), 766-788.
- Merton, R.K. "The Social Nature of Leadership," American Journal of Nursing, 69, 1969, p.2614-2618.
- Moss, S. A., & Ritossa, D. A. (2007).The impact of goal orientation on the association between leadership style and follower performance, creativity and work attitudes. Leadership & Organization Development Journal, 3(4), 433-456.
- Northouse, Peter G. (2001). *Leadership Theory and Practice*, second edition. Thousand Oaks, CA: Sage Publications, Inc.
- Peter Drucker, Practice of Management, Allied publishers, New Delhi, 1970, p.159.
- Rutherford, Donald (1992), Dictionary of Economics. Routledge,
- Ralph M. Stogdill, Handbook of Leadership: A Survey of Theory and Research, The Free Press, New York, 1974, p,7.
- Robbins, S. P., Judge, T. A. &Sanghi, S. (2007). Organizational Behavior. (12th ed.). India: Pearson: Prentice Hall.
- *Roget's 21st Century Thesaurus, Third Edition*. Philip Lief Group 2009. Web 07 Dec 2011.

- Osborn, Schermerhorn, & Hunt (2008). Organizational Behavior (10thed.). USA: John Wiley & Sons, Inc.
- Smith, G.P. (1997). The new leader: Bringing creativity and innovation to the workplace. Delray Beach, Florida: St. Lucie Press.
- Transactional and Laissez-Faire Leadership skills: A Meta-Analysis Comparing Women and Men. *Psychological Bulletin*, 129(4), 569-591.
- Yammarino, F.J., & Bass, B.M. (1990a). Transformational leadership and multiple levels of analysis. Human Relations, 43 (10), 975-995.
- Yammarino, F.J., & Bass, B.M. (1990b). Long-term forecasting of transformational leadership and its effects among naval officers: Some preliminary findings. In K.E. Clark & M.B. Clark (Eds.), Measures of Leadership (pp. 151-169). West Orange, N.J.: Leadership Library of America.
- Yukl, G. (1989). Managerial leadership: A review of theory and research. *Journal of Management*, 15, 251-289.
- Yukl, G. (2002). *Leadership in Organizations*. Prentice Hall: Upper Saddle River.
- Zenger Folkman. (2012). A Study in Leadership :Women do it Better than Me Nielsen, S., & Huse, M. 2010). The Contribution of Women on Boards of Directions: Going Beyond the Surface. *Corporate Governance: An International Review*, 18(2), 136-148.

# B


[1] Gibson, C.B., Conger, J. & Cooper, C. (1995). Perceptual Distance: the impact of differences in team leader and member perceptions across cultures. In W.H. Mobley (ed.) Advances in Global Leadership , 2:245-276.

[2] Deanne N. Den Hartog, Jaap J. Van Muijen and Paul L (1995)The Impact of Leader Behaviour on Trust in Management and Co-Workers. A Journal of Industrial Psychology, 2002, 28 (4), 29-34.

[3] Ivana Simic , (1998) ,"Transformational Leadership –The Key to Successful Management of Transformational Organizational Change ", The scientific Journal FACTA Universitatis Series : Economics And Organization , Vol. 1, No 6, 1998 pp . 49-55.

[4] Bernard M. Bass (1999) The Future of Leadership in Learning Organizations. Journal of Leadership & Organizational Studies. Vol 7, No.3, pp. 19-38.

[5] Gretchen Spreitzer and Kimberly Hopkins Perttula,(2001) Traditionality Matters: An Examination of the Effectiveness of Transformational Leadership in the U.S. and Taiwan. The Journal of Leadership Studies, 2, 3-18.

[6] Tracey T. Manning (2002) Legacy Leadership Institutes: Strengthening Leadership for Community Involvement in 50+ Adults. Journal of Leadership Education. Vol.5, issue, 2 pp. 80-92.

[7] Alice H. Eagly and Mary C. Johannesen, Marloes L. van Engen (2003) Transformational, Transactional, and Laissez-Faire Leadership Styles: A Meta-Analysis Comparing Women and Men. Psychological Bulletin. Vol, 129, No.4, pp.569-591.

[8] Boatwright et al (2003) Preferences for idealized styles of supervision. Leadership Quarterly, 13,327–342.

[9] Ken, W. Parry, S. B. P. (2003). Leadership, culture & performance: The case of the New Zeal& public sector: Journal of Change Management, v. 3, p. 376-399.

[10] Neubert, M. J., & Taggar, S. (2004). Pathways to informal leadership: The moderating role of gender on the relationship of individual differences and team member network centrality to informal leadership emergence. Leadership Quarterly, 15, 175-194.

[11] Hakan Erkutlu, (2006) "The impact of transformation al leadership on organizational and leadership effectiveness: The Turkish case", Journal of Management Development , Vol. 27 Iss: 7, pp.708 – 726.

[12] Alexi Matveev and Elean Lvina (2007) Intercultural Competence Assessment: What Are Its Key Dimensions Across Assessment Tools? Matveev.123-135.

[13] Hassan (2008)What we know about leadership. Review of General Psychology, 9 , 169-180.

[14] Jacqueline Whittred (2008) A qualitative exploration into the transformational leadership styles of senior police women. A Thesis. M.Sc. in Police Leadership and Management Department of Criminology, University of Leicester.

[15] Roger, J, G. (2008) "Transformational Leadership: The Impact on Organizational and Personal Outcomes", Emerging Leadership Journeys, Vol: 01, Issue: 01, PP: 4-24.

[16] Mahmood Ahmad Bodla and Muhammad Musarrat Nawaz (2010) Transformational Leadership Style and its Relationship with Satisfaction. Interdisciplinary Journal of Contemporary Research in Business. Vol, 2 No.1, pp. 371-381.

[17] Hassan, Rasool A. Fuwad, Bashir A. Rauf, Azam I. (2010) Pre-Training motivation and the Effectiveness of

Transformational Leadership Training: An experiment. Academy of Strategic Management Journal; Vol.9 Issue2, p1-8.

[18] Thomas W. Kent, Carrie A. Blair, Howard F. Rudd and Ulrich Schuele (2010) Gender Differences and Transformational Leadership Behavior: Do Both German Men and Women Lead in the Same Way? International Journal of Leadership Studies. Vol.6, Issue 1, pp. 52-66.

[19] Judeh (2010)Transformational Leadership: A Study of Gender Differences in Private Universities. International review of Business Research Papers, vol 6 (4), 118-125.

[20] Phondej et al (2010) Linking Female Leaders' Personality Traits to Motives, Powers and Behaviour Competencies: Women in Executive Level Positions. World Review of Business Research. Vol. 5. No. 3. Pp . 247 –258.

[21] Alpha and Vincent (2011) Assessment of Health–and Development -Promoting Leadership Behavior. $2^{nd}$ Canadian Conference on Positive Psychology.

[22] Muhammad Jamshed Khan and Naeem Aslam and Muhammad Naveed Riaz (2012) Leadership Styles as Predictors of Innovative Work Behavior. Pakistan Journal of Social and Clinical Psychology, Vol. 10 , No. 1, 17-22.

[23]Mahfuz Judeh (2012) Transformational Leadership: A Study of Gender Differences in Private Universities. International Review of Business Research Papers Volume 6. Number 4 Pp. 118-125.

[24]H. S Sandhu and Kanwaldeep Kaur (2010) Career Stage Effect on Organizational Commitment: Empirical Evidence from Indian Banking Industry International Journal of Business and Management Vol. 5, No. 12. Pp, 141-151.

[25]Boris Groysberg (2013) Empowering the Third Billion: Women and the World of Work in 2012. Retrieved

from http://www.booz.com/media/uploads/ BoozCo_Empowering -the-Third-Billion_Full-Report.pdf.

[26] Joris van der Voet (2013) The effectiveness and specificity of change management in a public organization: Transformational leadership and a bureaucratic organizational structure. European Management Journal.) xxx–xxx, pp.1-9.

[27] Nasiha Begu1, Farzand Ali Ja and Saif-Ud-Din Khan (2013) Women In Leadership: An Examination Of Transformational Leadership, Gender Role Orientation And Leadership Effectiveness. (A Case Study Of Pakistan And Turkey) Sarhd J. Agric. Vol.29, No.2, pp.307-316.

[28] Rupinder Kaur (2014) An Empirical Study of Transformational Leadership in Indian Banking Sector Volume : 3 | Issue : 2 | February 2014 · ISSN No 2277 - 8179

[29] Aarti Deveshwar and Indu Aneja (2014) A Study of Transnational And Transformation Leadership Styles and Factors Affect the Leadership Style. International Journal of Business, Economics and Management, 2014, 1 (8): 176-185.

[30] Naga Sai Sindhura Lakshmi Chaluvadi (2015) Differences in Leadership Styles between Genders: Outcomes and Effectiveness of Women in Leadership Roles. Johnson & Wales University.

# C


- Basow, S. A., & Rubenfeld, K. (2003). "Troubles talk": Effects of gender and gender typing.
- Croson, R. and Gneezy, U., 2009. Gender differences in preferences. Journal of Economic Literature 47, 448-474.
- Eagly, A. H., & Johnson, B. T (1990). Gender and leadership style. Psychological Bulletin 108(2),233-256
- Eagly, A.H. and M.C. Johannesen-Schmidt (2001): "The leadership Styles of Women and Men," Journal of Social Issues, 57, pp.781-797.
- Eckel, C.C. and Grossman, P.J., 2008. Men, Women, and Risk Aversion: Experimental Evidence. In C. Plott and V. Smith (Eds). Handbook of Experimental Economics Results, 1061– 1073. New York: Elsevier.
- Gray, J. (2004). Men are from Mars, Women are from Venus: The classic Guide to Undertanding the Opposite Sex. NY: HarperCollins Publishers.
- Maltz, D. N., & Borker, R. (1982). A cultural approach to male-female miscommunication. In J. J. Gumpertz (Ed.), Language and social identity. Cambridge; Cambridge University Press.
- Mason, E. S. (1994). Gender differences in job satisfaction. The Journal of Social Psychology, 135, 143-151.
- Turner, B. (2008). Does commitment develop in the same manner for male and female coaches? An examination of personal and job characteristic antecedents. Women in Sport & Physical Activity Journal, 17(1), 15.

# D

Aarti Deveshwar and Indu Aneja (2014) A Study of Transnational And Transformation Leadership Styles and Factors Affect the Leadership Style. International Journal of Business, Economics and Management, 2014, 1 (8): 176-185.


- Alexi Matveev and Elean Lvina (2007) Intercultural Competence Assessment: What Are Its Key Dimensions Across Assessment Tools? Matveev.123-135.
- Alice H. Eagly and Mary C. Johannesen, Marloes L. van Engen (2003) Transformational, Transactional, and Laissez-Faire Leadership Styles: A Meta-Analysis Comparing Women and Men. Psychological Bulletin. Vol, 129, No.4, pp. 569-591.
- Alimo-Metcalfe, B. & Alban-Metcalfe, J. (2001). 'The development of a new Transformational Leadership Questionnaire'. The Journal of Occupational & Organizational Psychology, 74, 1-27
- Alpha and Vincent (2011) Assessment of Health–and Development -Promoting Leadership Behavior. $2^{nd}$ Canadian Conference on Positive Psychology.
- Anderson, N., Lievens, F., van Dam, K., & Born, M. (2006). A construct-driven investigation of gender differences in leadership role assessment center. Journal of Applied Psychology, Vol 9, pp 555–566.
- Avolio, B. J., & Gardner, W. L. (2005). Authentic leadership development: Getting to the root of positive forms of leadership. The Leadership Quarterly, 16(3), pp 315-338.
- Bass, B. M. (1999) The Future of Leadership in Learning Organizations. Journal of Leadership & Organizational Studies. Vol 7, No.3, pp. 19-38.

- Basow, S. A., & Rubenfeld, K. (2003). "Troubles talk": Effects of gender and gender typing.
- Bernard M. Bass (1999) The Future of Leadership in Learning Organizations. Journal of Leadership & Organizational Studies. Vol 7, No.3, pp. 19-38.
- Boatwright et al (2003) Preferences for idealized styles of supervision. Leadership Quarterly, 13, pp 327–342.
- Carli, L. L. (1990). Gender, language, and influence. Journal of Personality and Social Psychology, Vol 59, pp 941–951.
- Chaluvadi, N. S. (2015) Differences in Leadership Styles between Genders: Outcomes and Effectiveness of Women in Leadership Roles. Johnson & Wales University.
- Croson, R. and Gneezy, U., 2009. Gender differences in preferences. Journal of Economic Literature 47, 448-474.
- Deanne N. Den Hartog, Jaap J. Van Muijen and Paul L (1995)The Impact of Leader Behaviour on Trust in Management and Co-Workers. A Journal of Industrial Psychology, 2002, 28 (4), 29-34.
- Eagly, A. H., & Johnson, B. T (1990). Gender and leadership style. Psychological Bulletin 108(2),233-256
- Eagly, A.H. and M.C. Johannesen-Schmidt (2001): "The leadership Styles of Women and Men," Journal of Social Issues, 57, pp.781-797.
- Erkutlu, H. (2006) "The impact of transformation al leadership on organizational and leadership effectiveness: The Turkish case", Journal of Management Development, Vol. 27 Iss: 7, pp.708 – 726.
- Fuwad, H., Rauf, B. And Azam, I. (2010) Pre-Training motivation and the Effectiveness of Transformational Leadership Training: An experiment. Academy of Strategic Management Journal; Vol.9 Issue2, pp 1-8.

- Gibson, C.B., Conger, J. And Cooper, C. (1995). Perceptual Distance: the impact of differences in team leader and member perceptions across cultures. In W.H. Mobley (ed.) Advances in Global Leadership , 2: pp245-276.
- Gray, J. (2004). Men are from Mars, Women are from Venus: The classic Guide to Undertanding the Opposite Sex. NY: HarperCollins Publishers.
- Gretchen Spreitzer and Kimberly Hopkins Perttula,(2001) Traditionality Matters: An Examination of the Effectiveness of Transformational Leadership in the U.S. and Taiwan. The Journal of Leadership Studies, 2, 3-18.
- Grint, K. (2005). Problems, problems, problems: The social construction of 'leadership'. Human Relations, 58(11), pp 1467-1494.
- H. S Sandhu and Kanwaldeep Kaur (2010) Career Stage Effect on Organizational Commitment: Empirical Evidence from Indian Banking Industry International Journal of Business and Management Vol. 5, No. 12. Pp, 141-151.
- Hakan Erkutlu, (2006) "The impact of transformation al leadership on organizational and leadership effectiveness: The Turkish case", Journal of Management Development , Vol. 27 Iss: 7, pp. 708 – 726.
- Hassan (2008)What we know about leadership. Review of General Psychology, 9 , 169-180.
- Hogg, M. A. (2001). A social identity theory of leadership. Personality and Social Psychology Review, Vol 5, pp 184–200.
- Ivana Simic , (1998) ,"Transformational Leadership –The Key to Successful Management of Transformational Organizational Change ", The scientific Journal FACTA Universitatis Series : Economics And Organization , Vol.

1, No 6, 1998 pp . 49-55.

- Jacqueline Whittred (2008) A qualitative exploration into the transformational leadership styles of senior police women. A Thesis. M.Sc. in Police Leadership and Management Department of Criminology, University of Leicester.
- Joris van der Voet (2013) The effectiveness and specificity of change management in a public organization: Transformational leadership and a bureaucratic organizational structure. European Management Journal.) xxx–xxx, pp.1-9.
- Judeh, M. (2012) Transformational Leadership: A Study of Gender Differences in Private Universities. International Review of Business Research Papers Volume 6 (4) 118-125.
- Kotlyar, I. & Karakowsky, L. (2006). Leading Conflict? Linkages Between Leader Behaviors and Group Conflict. Small Group Research, Vol. 37, No. 4, 377-403.
- Kotlyar, I., & Karakowsky, L. (2007). Falling Over Ourselves to Follow the Leader. Journal of Leadership & Organizational Studies, Vol. 14, No. 1, 38-49.
- Mahfuz Judeh (2012) Transformational Leadership: A Study of Gender Differences in Private Universities. International Review of Business Research Papers Volume 6. Number 4 Pp. 118-125.
- Mahmood Ahmad Bodla and Muhammad Musarrat Nawaz (2010) Transformational Leadership Style and its Relationship with Satisfaction. Interdisciplinary Journal of Contemporary Research in Business. Vol, 2 No.1, pp. 371-381.
- Maltz, D. N., & Borker, R. (1982). A cultural approach to male-female miscommunication. In J. J. Gumpertz (Ed.), Language and social identity. Cambridge; Cambridge

University Press.

- Mason, E. S. (1994). Gender differences in job satisfaction. The Journal of Social Psychology, 135, 143-151.
- Miller, J. B. (1976). Toward a new psychology of women. Boston: Beacon Press.
- Muhammad Jamshed Khan and Naeem Aslam and Muhammad Naveed Riaz (2012) Leadership Styles as Predictors of Innovative Work Behavior. Pakistan Journal of Social and Clinical Psychology, Vol. 10 , No. 1, 17-22.
- Naga Sai Sindhura Lakshmi Chaluvadi (2015) Differences in Leadership Styles between Genders: Outcomes and Effectiveness of Women in Leadership Roles. Johnson & Wales University.
- Nasiha Begu1, Farzand Ali Ja and Saif-Ud-Din Khan (2013) Women In Leadership: An Examination Of Transformational Leadership, Gender Role Orientation And Leadership Effectiveness. (A Case Study Of Pakistan And Turkey) Sarhd J. Agric. Vol.29, No.2, pp.307-316.
- Neubert, M. J., & Taggar, S. (2004). Pathways to informal leadership: The moderating role of gender on the relationship of individual differences and team member network centrality to informal leadership emergence. Leadership Quarterly, 15, 175-194.
- Pielstick, C.D. (1998). The transforming leader: A meta-ethnographic analysis. *Community College Review*, 26(3), 15-34.
- Phondej et al (2010) Linking Female Leaders' Personality Traits to Motives, Powers and Behaviour Competencies: Women in Executive Level Positions. World Review of Business Research. Vol. 5. No. 3. Pp . 247 –258.
- Roger, J, G. (2008) "Transformational Leadership: The

Impact on Organizational and Personal Outcomes", Emerging Leadership Journeys, Vol: 01, Issue: 01, pp 4-24.

- Thomas W. Kent, Carrie A. Blair, Howard F. Rudd and Ulrich Schuele (2010) Gender Differences and Transformational Leadership Behavior: Do Both German Men and Women Lead in the Same Way? International Journal of Leadership Studies. Vol.6, Issue 1, pp. 52-66.

- Tracey T. Manning (2002) Legacy Leadership Institutes: Strengthening Leadership for Community Involvement in 50+ Adults. Journal of Leadership Education. Vol.5, issue, 2 pp. 80-92.

- Turner, B. (2008). Does commitment develop in the same manner for male and female coaches? An examination of personal and job characteristic antecedents. Women in Sport & Physical Activity Journal, 17(1), 15.